BRAI
LONGER

T

PEAK DISTRICT

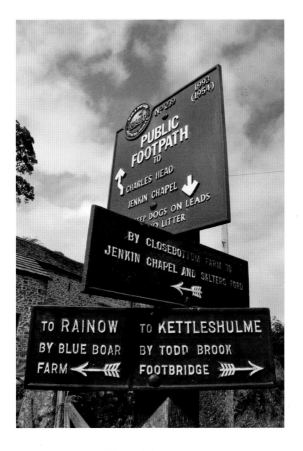

NEIL COATES

BRADWELL
BOOKS

Published by Bradwell Books
9 Orgreave Close Sheffield S13 9NP
Email: books@bradwellbooks.co.uk

British Library Cataloguing in Publication Data: a catalogue record for this book is available from the British Library.

1st Edition

ISBN: 9781910551677

Print: Hobbs the Printers, Totton Hants

Design by: Mark Titterton

Typesetting by: Mark Titterton

Photograph Credits: © Neil Coates

Maps: Contain Ordnance Survey data
© Crown copyright and database right 2016

Ordnance Survey licence number 100039353

The information in this book has been produced in good faith and is intended as a general guide. Bradwell Books and its authors have made all reasonable efforts to ensure that the details are correct at the time of publication. Bradwell Books and the author cannot accept any responsibility for any changes that have taken place subsequent to the book being published. It is the responsibility of individuals undertaking any of the walks listed in this publication to exercise due care and consideration for the health and wellbeing of each other in the party. Particular care should be taken if you are inexperienced.

ACCESS LAND RESTRICTIONS

Some walks use access to land granted under the Countryside & Rights of Way Act 2000. For a few days each year (usually between May and October) access may be suspended. If this possibility is noted in the introduction to the walk, refer to the website **peakdistrict.gov.uk** and follow the link to 'Access Land Restrictions' which will detail any such closures.

CONTENTS

ENGLAND'S FIRST NATIONAL PARK (1951) STANDS ASTRIDE THE SOUTHERNMOST HILLS, VALES AND MOORS OF THE SOUTHERN PENNINES. BOUNDED BY CITIES SUCH AS MANCHESTER, SHEFFIELD AND STOKE, THE PEAK DISTRICT WAS A CRADLE OF THE INDUSTRIAL REVOLUTION. SUCH A HEADY MIX OF SOCIAL HERITAGE AND MORPHOLOGICAL DIVERSITY PROVIDES FOR SOME OF THE MOST MEMORABLE COUNTRYSIDE EXPERIENCES IN THE LAND.

It was here that the famous 'mass trespass' of 1932 accelerated the train of events which resulted in national parks and greater access to the countryside for all. Today's rights of way were yesterday's paths to work and yesteryear's transport network. By walking these, we're perpetuating a centuries old birthright to the great outdoors.

The area has astonishingly varied landscapes and landforms, resulting from the differing underlying geology. At its heart, the White Peak plateau is a gentler, greener realm dappled with pastureland, ashwoods and cleaved by astonishing gorges sliced into the pale limestone. Its straw-coloured hamlets and wildflower-drifted byways amidst filigree walls are the epitome of rural England. The enfolding horseshoe of

darker uplands is a brooding borderland of remote, reedy moors bounded by craggy edges with endless views and lively, tumbling streams - the enticing gritstone countryside of the Dark Peak with its archetypical weaving villages, salters' ways and secluded farmsteads.

The walks in this book make the most of such variety. Some visit favourite places and locations, often approaching on paths and byways less-travelled; others seek out the more tranquil corners away from the crowds, opening up new vistas and experiences that relatively few visitors discover. Chance to nibble at the fringes; tackle wildflower-rich towpaths, deserted mine tracks and grassy trods redolent of a quieter time when the National Park was young.

Delightful diversity is guaranteed.

The Walks

All these routes should be achievable by any rambler of average fitness. Short, very steep ascents and descents; stepping stones; rocky paths; marshy sections; ledged paths and high undergrowth may be encountered. In general, longer walks will be more challenging. Each route is graded according to difficulty.

EASY – walks have very few steep or awkward sections; but do expect some modest climbs and descents peppered with a few more adventurous stretches.

MODERATE – walks include generally more sustained steeper sections; more climbing and may include long stretches of steps and/or encounter very uneven ground.

CHALLENGING – walks include some rough going and lots of ups and downs, some of which are particularly steep or lengthy and require care and judgement to be exercised.

All walks use public rights of way, concessionary routes or access land. They may need perseverance to follow as their maintenance is variable - loose stiles, awkward gates or dense vegetation for example. Any known difficulties are mentioned; but some may disappear or new ones occur.

Take heed of the weather and likely challenges along the route; dress accordingly and wear sturdy footwear. Your safety is your own responsibility - take a few sensible precautions and be circumspect when choosing and using a route.

WALK BETWEEN TWO CONTRASTING LIMESTONE VILLAGES WITH PLAGUE AND SPA HERITAGE AND SOME FINE VIEWS.

The tale of strong leadership, self-sacrifice and tragedy at Eyam is widely known and rightly feted. When plague-lice-infested cloth arrived at the village from London in 1665, William Mompesson, the local parson, persuaded the villagers to cut themselves off from the surrounding villages and farms in order to try to stem the spread of the deadly disease. This selfless, ultimately successful, gesture cost the lives of nearly half of the villagers but saved countless others. Those dark days are well documented and celebrated at locations across this pretty village spread below Eyam Edge. On the last Sunday each August a memorial service is held in the village to remember the victims; it's at Cucklett Delf, where Mompesson held outdoor services when the church was closed.

Just a mile away, the compact village of Stoney Middleton plugs the foot of wooded Middleton Dale and fully lives up to its name, with a series of old and current quarries nibbling away at the rich limestone deposits in the gorges and hills above. It once had a different *raison d'être*, however. The Romans came seeking lead here and also found a hot spring with water issuing at a constant temperature. They may have lingered and bathed here; a more concerted effort to establish a spa was made in Georgian times.

This walk sidles between these two very different villages, offering chance to discover the distinctive heritage of both places. Starting from Eyam, the route first climbs steeply through woodlands before an elevated country lane offers a wonderful viewing platform over a wide swathe of the southern areas of the Peak District. Old mining tracks and byways delve deeper into the secluded countryside behind Derbyshire's highest pub before an ancient way takes us towards one of the area's old lead mines and the memorial of Mompesson's Well.

Dropping past some of the poignant plague-victim graves, the way slides down through woods and haymeadows to reach Stoney Middleton's village centre with its unusual church and partially restored bath-house close to the village wells, 'dressed' in summer with memorable creations of petals, seeds, fruits and twigs.

Clipping through the old village, the path then climbs through meadows and past an old plague stone before reaching the Lydgate tombs in Eyam. There's chance to explore the village's church before reaching the Old Hall and the plague houses. In season there are a couple of well dressings here, too.

THE BASICS

Distance: 6¾ miles / 10.9km

Gradient: Undulating, with several steady climbs and descents

Severity: Easy

Approx. time to walk: 4 hours

Stiles: About 5 plus several gates

Map: OS Explorer OL24 (The Peak District: White Peak Area)

Path description: Field paths and tracks, byways, tarred lanes

Start Point: Eyam village, opposite museum (GR SK 215767)

Parking: Village car park, Hawkhill Road, Eyam (free) (S32 5QP)

Dog friendly: Only suitable for agile and fit dogs

Public toilets: At start

Nearest refreshment: Pubs and tearooms in Eyam; pub in Stoney Middleton

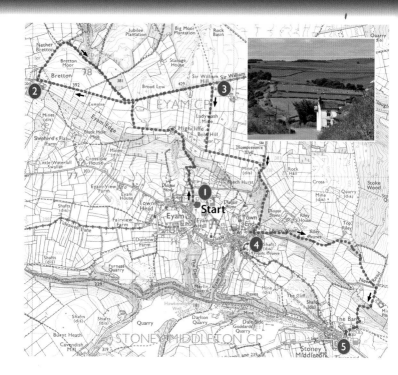

The Route

1. Turn uphill from the car park and walk to the bend, where 'The Nook' is the way to take to the left. Beyond houses this roughens and steepens as it rises through woodland covering Eyam Edge to reach a tarred lane. Bear left and remain true to it for 1.5km (1 mile), rounding several bends and enjoying a huge panoramic view before reaching The Barrel Inn at Bretton. A handful of drovers' and packhorse routes converge here; the inn dates from 1597 and originated as a service station for these early hauliers.

2. Take the lane that turns up right beside the inn, then drops gently towards the narrow valleys of Bretton and Abney Cloughs, sliced deeply into the undulating moorland plateau here. Where the lane fails at 'The Croft' cottage, continue up the rough byway, regaining a little height across Bretton Moor, presently reaching a tarred lane. Turn left; then at the bend keep ahead on the rougher way, Sir William Hill Road. This very ancient route became the main turnpike road across this part of Derbyshire sometime in the early 1700s and is probably named after a local landowner, either Sir William Saville of Eyam or Sir William Cavendish, owner of a nearby estate. The way undulates easily along the ridge, rewarded with superlative views across both White and Dark Peaks. Remain with this to pass by the hill-top aerial on your right. In a further 175m a fingerposted path crosses the old trackway.

3. Take the stone stile to the right and walk the grassy path beside the wall. On your left is the chimney at Ladywash Mine, a lead mine that eventually closed in the 1990s as a fluorspar works. At the next lane turn left and track it downhill to the T-junction in 600m.

    The way is right; but first divert left the 100m to Mompesson's Well on the left, a poignant reminder of the Great Plague. An information board tells the story here. Return downhill to the junction and keep ahead to pass by the drive to Hollowbrook Barn. In another few paces take the gap-stile on the left, joining a woodland path for Eyam down through Hollow Brook Wood. This reaches cottages at the edge of Eyam and advances to a road junction opposite an old chapel.

4. Turn left uphill, walking the 100m to a fork where the way is left along Riley Lane, passing a signpost for Riley Graves. These are another reminder of the pestilence that decimated the village, and are found in a walled enclosure in the pasture to your left in 600m, beyond the woods and the side lane for Riley Farm (which you ignore). The graves are those of the Hancock family.

    Carry on along the lane, enjoying some grand views down the Derwent Valley. The lane becomes grass-centred. As you reach the next stand of woodland in 300m take the signed byway to the right. At the waymarked junction in 200m fork right, soon joining an enclosed track between haymeadows down to a road at a sharp bend. Cross into the rough track behind the chevron sign opposite, which curls down through a stand of woodland as an occasionally awkward-underfoot track, to reach a tarred lane at the edge of Stoney Middleton.

    On your right shortly is the bath-house. The Romans discovered the warm spring here and doubtless indulged in its constant 63°F flow of water for medicinal purposes. Many centuries later the local landowner, Thomas Denman, sought to develop the waters as a spa in Georgian times but with only limited success. The plaque here details the heritage of this rather obscure site.

    At the nearby corner is one of the village wells which are 'dressed' each July. A little further on is St Martin's Church, with its very unusual octagonal nave. Dating from 1759, it was designed by the architect James Paine, who also designed the stable blocks and the Derwent Bridge at Chatsworth House. Continue round the bend above the brook to reach a T-junction opposite one of the village's many lost pubs, which served the miners, shoemakers and quarrymen who worked in this once-thriving old village.

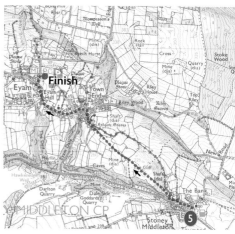

5. There's an open pub, The Moon, off to the left across the busy main road; otherwise turn right up the steep tarred lane, 'The Bank', to reach its summit. Here slip right into the 'No Through Road' and then keep immediately left up Cliff Bottom. This climbs past further old cottages to reach a sign 'Unsuitable for Motor  Vehicles'. Just past this take the signed handgate to the left, commencing a grassy climb up the long pasture. In about 300m, beside trees, you'll reach a plague stone, in the top of which is a series of holes. This is one of the spots around Eyam where coins were left in vinegar-filled holes in payment for goods that outsiders left for the quarantined folk of the village. The vinegar was believed to kill the plague.

The field path becomes a walled path beyond a stile. Advance on the well-defined way, soon reaching houses at the edge of Eyam. Keep ahead through the gates and along the tarred lane of Lydgate. Another brace of walled graves are on your left shortly before the main street is reached. To your right is the site of one of the village's two well dressings, dressed at the start of the Wakes Week at the end of August.

This is Town End, where the village inn, The Miner's Arms, is tucked away up a side street. It recalls the most important local industry in centuries past; lead mining. The Romans possibly first worked the ore here; by the 15th century it was a major employer in the area and remained so until late Victorian times. The main mines, north of the village, were up to 1,000 feet (300m) deep. Within living memory fluorspar was worked from some of the older mines and spoil tips. Other industries included silk spinning and printing, and shoe-making, which employed up to 200 people until the 1950s.

Cross left over The Square, passing the bus shelter and climbing gently up Church Street. The village church, St Lawrence's, has much information about the plague story. Of a much earlier period, look for the spectacularly decorated Celtic Cross in the churchyard, dating from the time in which the original church here was founded.

Plenty of information boards throughout the long village detail the events of the Great Plague and its arrival in the village, carried on fleas infesting cloth imported from London, where the pestilence was already rife. Plague stones and victims' cottages all add to the jigsaw here. The very imposing Eyam Hall was built just after the plague's devastating visitation on the village. The building and land were a generous wedding present to John Wright; the place remains in the Wright family today, although now leased to the National Trust and open most days (not Mondays) to visitors.

Not far past the green and village stocks is the turn, right, back to the car park.

FROM A TRANQUIL WHITE PEAK VILLAGE INTO AN
ASTONISHING GORGE WHERE A FAMOUS BOOK WAS INSPIRED.

Home to fewer than 300 residents, the
compact little settlement of Alstonefield
slumbers around a clutch of village greens
that ripple between an ancient church and
the old high road which threads across
the rich pastureland of this corner of
Staffordshire. It's one of those out-of-the-
way places that are always a delight to
happen across, and is located amidst some
of the very best, if relatively unknown,
limestone scenery in the National Park.

Commencing from the village, this walk
threads through a series of the small fields
that characterise the farms here before
dropping into secluded Narrowdale and its
abandoned hamlet huddled amidst grassy
knolls. This is a very secret place, with old
walled tracks dissipating into ghostly fields
still grazed by contented cattle; marshy,
wildflower-rich hollows alive with summer
butterflies and tantalising views across a
landscape of haymeadows and high pasture
seemingly unchanging across the decades.

The route advances to reach the end of a tarred lane beside the vigorous waters of
the River Dove, a remote spot plugged by thick woodland billowing from the mouth of
Beresford Dale. It's here that the 17th-century gentlemen-of-leisure Charles Cotton and
Izaak Walton used to meet, relax and fish in the languid pools and swift rapids of the Dove.
Their exploits form the basis of Walton's *Compleat Angler* book, first published in 1653 and
rarely out of print since; it's said to be the most frequently reprinted book in the English
language apart from the Bible. This sometimes jocular commentary on fishing and other
country pursuits was written, at least in part, in a fishing lodge that still exists (on private
land) higher up the valley.

The route turns away from this Arcadia to pursue a course beside the Dove into the most
astonishing, canyon-like valley of Wolfscote Dale, essentially one of the upper branches of
the much more renowned Dovedale. There's a decent path all the way, passing weirs, huge

buttresses of limestone, towering crags, pinnacles and secluded side valleys before reaching the hamlet of Milldale, clustered above its ancient packhorse bridge. Hidden deep in this jigsaw of gorges and dales, the way out is an initially steep path that gains the plateau top and winds through more rippling wildflower meadows to return to Alstonefield and its welcoming inn.

THE BASICS

Distance: 6½ miles / 10.5km

Gradient: Undulating; one short steep pitch

Severity: Easy

Approx. time to walk: 3¾ hours

Stiles: Three plus several handgates

Map: OS Explorer OL24 (The Peak District: White Peak Area)

Path description: Compacted paths, field paths and tracks, tarred lanes, may be muddy in places

Start Point: Alstonefield (GR SK 131556)

Parking: Free car parks in the village (DE6 2FY)

Dog friendly: Only suitable for agile and fit dogs

Public toilets: At start and in Milldale

Nearest refreshment: Pub at start, seasonal and weekend refreshments at Milldale

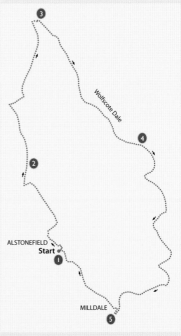

The Route

1. Find The George Inn beside the largest of the village greens here. Put the pub to your back and turn left to the nearby junction. Head left here before bearing right (sign for 'Toilets') along the lane, shortly keeping ahead at the next junction with road signs for Hulme End and Hartington. Almost immediately after this junction, with the old village pump to your left, fork right up the minor road to the right of the little triangular green. Walk the 50 or so paces to the next tiny green; here turn right along the 'No Through Road', which soon roughens beyond cottages. At the nearby three gates, choose the middle one and trace the grass-centred track round the easy left bend; then at the succeeding right bend it's time to leave this track.

    Turn left to the waymarked handgate beneath an enormous ash tree. The field-edge path now passes through a series of small fields interspersed by more handgates. As the wall turns left after the fifth handgate, keep straight ahead across the oddly-shaped pasture to a further gate some 50m up from a small stable. Continue ahead to a stone-step stile near a ruined building; climb the stile and then turn left, field-side, to reach a roadside handgate.

Don't use this; instead turn sharply right and cut across pastures towards the right-hand corner of the distant copse of trees. There's a very narrow gap-stile to use here, then walk left of the dew pond to the handgate into a walled field road.

2. Obey the fingerpost for Narrowdale and cross directly over the track, picking up the defined path across a narrow pasture then ahead, aiming just right of the distant lone tree via a handgate in an offset corner. Walk beside the wall (left) to the point beyond the tree where another thin gap-stile, this one with a huge upright stone, offers passage through a cross-wall. The path now advances along a developing notch in the hillside, very gradually dropping to meet a wall coming in at a fine angle from your right. Simply keep this on your right, with grand views ahead across the higher Dove Valley. The path reaches a heavy field gate, beyond which you drop to the nearby cluster of buildings at Narrowdale.

Sheltered by trees is a melancholic collection of barns and abandoned farmhouses. For over 600 years the hamlet was home to the descendants of one family before they sold up about a century ago. The farm remained inhabited until the early years of this century, since when one of the old farmyards has been used as a cattle pen; another is a ghostly recollection of busier times, with rusting old farm machinery frozen in time, overlooked by the windows of a solid, derelict farmhouse.

The way is to the right at the junction of tracks amidst the buildings. You'll pass below a high old stone retaining wall, then ahead through a gate and along the walled track away from the buildings. Where the better track strikes ahead and uphill at the near end of a small side-dale in 150m, you instead should bend left alongside the wall. Beyond a bridgelate the way becomes better defined, developing into a pleasant old farm lane, lined with mature trees. Several further gates draw this old way gradually down towards Beresford Dale; in early/midsummer the track is generously lined by great drifts of bright blue meadow cranesbill, whilst damper hollows glow with fragrant meadowsweet. At the fingerpost, keep ahead through the handgate for Hulme End, advancing on the improving track to reach a narrow tarred lane beyond gates. Turn right to its nearby end amidst riverside trees.

3. This is the lower end of the wooded Beresford Dale. Our route crosses the narrow, angled footbridge across the River Dove here. The fishing lodge where Izaak Walton fished and contemplated is upstream beyond the woods; the woods themselves cover the site of the long-demolished Beresford Hall, where Walton's companion Charles Cotton lived. Once across the bridge turn downstream across the water meadow, soon reaching handgates and a footbridge. Don't cross this, but continue downstream, keeping the Dove on your right.

    The character of the walk immediately changes as it enters the highest reaches of Wolfscote Dale. The valley sides steepen, soon becoming craggy cliffs with great scree slopes of fallen rock plunging down to the river's edge. It's magnificent walking on a good path. The river is bordered by strands of alder and summer blooms of huge butterbur leaves, like patches of gigantic rhubarb. Look for water crowfoot spangling the river in midsummer.

4. Continuing downstream past small weirs, in 1.5km (1 mile) the narrow mouth of Biggin Dale is passed on the left, just beyond a wooden gate. For much of the year this is a dry valley; only in the wettest weather does a temporary stream flow into the Dove here.

    Shortly past this point ash woods appear as a green cloak clothing the precipitous sides of the dale. Pass by several footbridges, always remaining true to the path on the left of the Dove. About 1km (¾ mile) past Coldeaton footbridge (and stone hut) a secluded house is reached, opposite which is a sturdy old mill. Cross the narrow road bridge here and fork left on the lane signed for Milldale. A pavement accompanies this down above the river, presently reaching the hamlet of Milldale.

The oldest structure here is probably the packhorse bridge, Viator's Bridge, across the Dove. Nearby is a small stone barn, once stables for the long-gone mill and now an information point where the heritage of the little settlement is detailed. Corn, ochre and calamine were all ground in the mill here at one time or another.

5. Leave along the narrow side lane (signed for the chapel) which passes the seasonal refreshment shop, Polly's Cottage, and then the red telephone box on your left. Walk up the lane for about 100m to find the driveway, left, to Valley View. Enter the grounds, looking for the handgated path through an arch in the cupressus hedge. Head from this to a handgate in a cross-wall. Continue beyond this up below the line of cables, a short but steep climb which levels at the break of slope where the onward direction is to veer right to find a narrow gap-stile in the far-right corner.

Look for the distant tower of Alstonefield's church and aim across the next meadow slightly to the left of this, using a handgate through the intervening cross-wall. Now curve right to reach a lane at the right-hand margin of the trees surrounding the churchyard.

Turn left back to the village. It's well worth popping into St Peter's Church here, which was founded in 892 and has some fine wood carvings on pulpit and box pews. The George Inn is nearby.

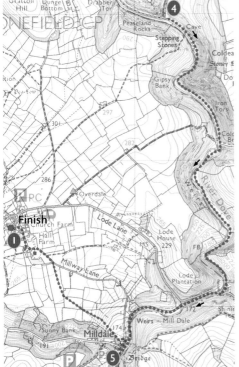

Walk the lesser-visited side of the Derwent Valley to extraordinary viewpoints and a geomorphological oddity below rolling grouse moors.

The Upper Derwent Valley is one of the familiar images of the National Park. Ladybower, Upper Derwent and Howden Reservoirs are a popular playground for active visitors cycling the waterside lane and rougher tracks that circuit the lakes, whilst gentle woodland walks attract families seeking short strolls in this beautiful crease in the vast moors of High Peak. This is also some of England's most remote and forbidding upland country; the parish of shooting parties, bog-trotter walkers and determined birdwatchers seeking some of the rare species that make the area home.

This walk explores part of the lesser known western side of the Derwent's convoluted uplands. It starts beside Ladybower Reservoir above where Derwent village once stood. This was submerged beneath the waters of the reservoir in the 1940s; all that remain are a few of the higher farms and the War Memorial, beside the road just south of the car park. The route rises through fir woods cloaking the steep sides of the valley before emerging onto a modest ridge which separates the valleys of the Derwent and Ashop rivers.

Exquisite views are the reward for this modest effort; and they are views shared with relatively few on this unfashionable side of the Derwent's highest reaches. There's a saying that the Peak District doesn't really have any peaks. The views from this ridge-top all but give the lie to this. The panorama across to the Vale of Edale and the immense bulk of Kinder Scout offers a rolling series of snouts and crags, ends and tors that bristle the landscape; modest peaks of perfection in a sublime and tranquil countryside. Birdwatchers can be in their element here, with golden plover and short-eared owls as well as the chance of peregrine falcons and ravens.

The high point of the walk is the ridge and crags above Alport hamlet. This series of cliffs, canyons and bluffs results from land-heave and slippage over thousands of years. It's an astonishing location, backed by superb vistas to the highest moors and edges.

From here the route descends across grouse moor to fall to the flooded Derwent Valley beside the highest of the reservoirs. On tranquil days the view across to the dam is like an enormous infinity pool, with purple moors a stunning backdrop. Below Howden Dam is the site of Birchinlee, or Tin Town; interpretation boards here detail the absorbing history of this temporary town that disappeared over a century ago.

THE BASICS

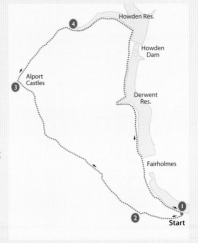

Distance: 9 miles / 14.5km

Gradient: One steady climb, otherwise gently undulating

Severity: Easy

Approx. time to walk: 5 hours

Stiles: Three plus several handgates

Map: OS Explorer OL1 (The Peak District: Dark Peak Area)

Path description: Woodland and moorland paths and tracks, tarred lanes

Start Point: Ladybower Reservoir (GR SK 180885)

Parking: Bridge End car park (fee) or nearby lay-bys (free) beside minor road for Derwent Valley Dams (S33 0AQ)

Dog friendly: Only suitable for agile and fit dogs

Public toilets: Fairholmes

Nearest refreshment: refreshment kiosk at Fairholmes; Ladybower Inn at Ashopton is 2½ miles / 4km away from start

(NB: check Access Land closure information – see p.2)

3 ALPORT CASTLES AND DERWENT VALLEY

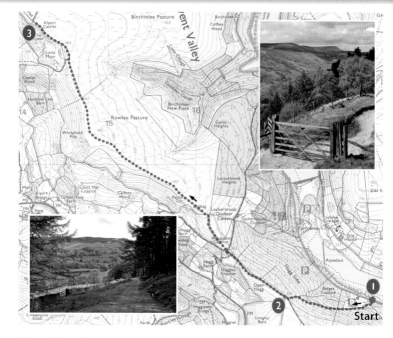

The Route

1. Look for the signed bridleway which starts from a gate at the southern end of the Bridge End car park – if you've parked in the lay-by then return along the road to this point. Pick up this stony track, initially rising beside the trees and then through the conifer plantations and broadleaf woods that cover the slopes of Hagg Side. It's a gradual climb for 1km (¾ mile) before a field gate marks the top end of the woodlands at the ridge crest. Use the handgate on your right, joining a well-defined path beside the strand of old pine trees at the top of the rough sloping pasture.

    There are marvellous views to the west and north from this easy-going largely grassy trod. Back to your left above the fringe of trees marking the deep, hidden Woodlands Valley (and main A57 road), the sharp cliff face is Back Tor, high above Castleton. The shapely top with the prominent path is Mam Tor, whilst the long, muscular ridge leading away is Rushup Edge. Looking ahead as you walk is the memorable scarp marking the edge of the high plateau of Kinder Scout, culminating in the craggy snout of Fairbrook Naze. It's one of the most appealing and attractive views in the Dark Peak, yet you may have it largely to yourself, as few visitors to the Derbyshire Lake District make it far from the waterside paths and road.

2. Advance along the good path; in 750m you'll reach a junction at a woodland corner just beyond a gate and stile. Look directly ahead up the hillside to locate the high ladder-stile straddling a wall 100m distant, just left of the trees breaking the skyline. Cross over the intervening stony roadway and up a grassy path to this

20

stile (next to a gate). Beyond it keep ahead along the gently rising field, keeping parallel to the wall on your left. Climb another stile at the far end; then bear left to pick up the good path past the National Trust sign for Rowlee Pasture. Look back here for a final view of Ladybower Reservoir in the valley bottom.

It's a good path, possibly boggy in patches, that soon becomes the easiest of walks above the break of slope above Woodlands Valley as it's been paved for the best part of 1km. Passing high above Rowlee Farm, the delectable view up Woodlands Valley is replaced by one down into the secluded valley of Alport Dale as the path gradually eases right and northwards along the fringe of Rowlee Pasture. It's open moorland, with views stretching across a patchwork of mottled browns and yellow, greens and olives to the heart of the immense tract of mosses, moors and cloughs of the deepest High Peak. Allow your gaze to drift back-right to some of the great gritstone scarps of the Dark Peak – Derwent, Bamford and Stanage Edges.

The paved section ends as the well-defined path passes through the line of a tumbled wall; here keep ahead alongside another ruinous wall. Ahead of you, the interlocking spurs of Alport Dale take the eye to the distant long horizon of Bleaklow, with the serrated snout of Bleaklow Head just visible as its left-hand end. The few buildings down in the valley far below are those at Alport hamlet. The steep slopes to your left now become dramatically fractured as the site of the tremendous landslip of Alport Castles is reached.

It's a rugged terrain, slightly reminiscent of the mesas and canyons familiar from many Western films. It's thought to have formed after the last ice age, when unstable beds of rock gave way in a spectacular rotational landslip around 8,500 years ago. The largest such morphological feature in England, it's one of the Peaks' hidden landscapes. There's a tarn below, perched on a ledge high above the impressive depths of the Alport Valley. The drops here are precipitous, so tread warily and stay back from the edges.

Keep ahead, where there may be a camouflaged hide perched close to the edge. This is sited to allow users views of peregrine falcons which are known to nest here. It's also a reliable place to watch ravens, which also nest on the inaccessible crags and soar in the breezes swirling off the rocks. Staying on the path a short distance further brings you to a point immediately above The Tower, one of the most memorable features here. The tarn may be glimpsed below this.

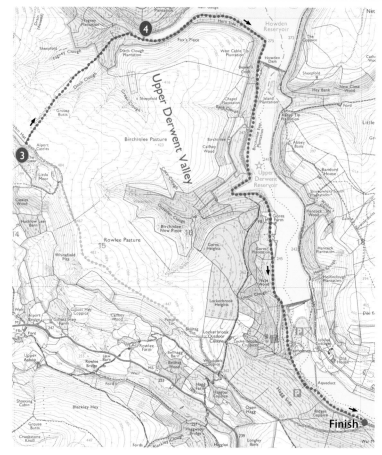

3. You'll immediately reach the stub-end of a derelict wall, whilst a broken wall continues ahead along the edge. The way is to the right here, directly away from the edge and wall along a path which in 200m develops into a shooters' track. The way declines gradually, slinking through a line of grouse butts. Keep to the line on the left of the developing little clough; the track forges ahead along the crest of a small ridge as it drops gently towards the woodland of Ditch Clough Plantation. Glimpses of Howden Reservoir deep in the

Derwent Valley are had before the track reaches a gate and handgate into the woods. Follow the track down through the trees, a delightful stretch of beechwoods and pines flanked by fir plantations. At the slope foot turn right on the firmer, wider track along the valley of the little River Westend to reach a tarred lane which rounds the edge of an arm of Howden Reservoir.

4. Turn right along this, putting the lake on your left. This is the earliest of the three gigantic reservoirs which drown the higher reaches of the Derwent Valley. Howden took 11 years to complete and fill, with work starting in 1901.

It's now simply a matter of following the road. Huge efforts have been made to clear rhododendrons from the steep banks of the reservoir, opening up views of the waters as foreground to the high, rounded edges to the east and north. Stay with the road past the dam, below which the valley is soon filled again by the higher reaches of the Upper Derwent Reservoir. Look out on the left for a small structure behind a bus-stop pole. This is the first of a series that reveal the fascinating history of 'Tin Town', where the builders of the valley's upper two dams lived. The bus-stop pole is a stage on the summer weekend minibus service which uses the lane up the valley, when cars are banned.

Beyond Upper Derwent Dam you'll pass by the entrance to the Fairholmes Visitor Centre complex. Just after this, a footpath on the left avoids the road for the next 1km, running above Ladybower Reservoir to return to Bridge End car park.

EXPLORE SHAPELY CRAGS, STANDING STONES AND A HERMIT'S RETREAT IN A GRITSTONE CORNER OF THE WHITE PEAK.

Birchover nestles in the undulating hill country to the west of Matlock. It's little more than a strand of cottages and byways straddling the slopes falling from the rippling heather upland of Stanton Moor. One of a string of pretty stone villages in the area, its two pubs and network of paths have long been favourites of walkers seeking the quieter side of the Peak District. Spread liberally across the local countryside is a generous selection of ancient sites and intriguing geomorphological features; many with tantalising or mysterious origins. This walk links together several of these.

Just above the village's Druid Inn are Rowtor Rocks. This modest eruption of gritstone is riddled by clefts, steps, carvings and viewpoints, many of which were created by a former local rector, Thomas Eyre, to celebrate the 'Glorious Revolution' of 1688 and the accession to the throne of William III and Queen Mary. Well-used concessionary paths give access to this tree-hidden playground; it's popular with boulderers and scramblers – beware sheer drops.

Paths and tracks drop from the village into the little valley of Ivy Bar Brook, then climb again to the striking crags of Cratcliff, an area of Access Land split by the Limestone Way footpath. One of the hollows in the cliff holds a medieval crucifixion carving. The Hermit's Cave was

long home to men leading a troglodyte-like existence; they were often in the service of the local abbey or church and paid a small stipend by such.

Across the hillside is the bold outline of the gritstone tors at Mock Beggars Hall. These bristling pinnacles are also called Robin Hood's Stride, although any connection to the medieval folk hero and rogue is perhaps as fanciful as the man in Lincoln green himself. The walk allows exploration of these shapely spires before progressing to the village of Elton. Once a centre of the lead-mining industry, it's now a tranquil backwater, whilst the village pub is one of the least-altered in the country and features in the CAMRA National Inventory of Pub Interiors – the Oscars of the pub heritage world!

Cutting back below Birchover, the walk then advances across Stanton Moor, renowned as a Bronze Age necropolis with dozens of burial mounds and cists. Passing a Georgian folly tower, the way then loops past a fine stone circle before encountering the mysterious Cork Stone, returning to Birchover through cool woods.

THE BASICS

Distance: 7 miles / 11.3km

Gradient: Undulating, with several steady climbs

Severity: Easy

Approx. time to walk: 4½ hours

Stiles: Many and varied, plus many handgates

Map: OS Explorer OL24 (The Peak District: White Peak Area)

Path description: Field and farm tracks and paths, tarred lanes, moorland paths

Start Point: Birchover (GR SK 237622)

Parking: Roadside parking with consideration (DE4 2BN)

Dog friendly: Only suitable for agile and fit dogs

Public toilets: Birchover

Nearest refreshment: Two pubs in Birchover; pub in Elton has very limited opening times

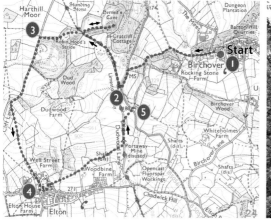 

The Route

1. Find The Druid Inn at the bottom of the village and take the narrow lane to its left. Just past the pub's grounds, a path on the right is the diversion to Rowtor Rocks. A little further down the lane is the tiny village church of St Michael, built 300 years ago as the private chapel to long-demolished Rowtor Hall. At the junction by the Old Vicarage, keep ahead on the track for Rocking Stone Farm. At the left-hairpin bend, cut straight ahead along the rougher track below woods, ignoring the nearby waymarked handgate. Climb a stile; then 50m beyond the part-ruined barn fork right over the stile/gate onto a steep path down the scrubby hillside to railings and a handgate onto a road. Turn left and walk downhill for 150m to a turn on the right.

2. Turn into the lane and immediately take the gated track right, marked with a Limestone Way fingerpost. This strikes gently uphill, presently bending right towards a house nestling beneath the crags of Cratcliff. At this bend leave the driveway and fork left up the fingerposted Limestone Way. Use the left-hand handgate and climb past trees to a fingerpost.

   First, turn right over the high stile onto the path to the far end of the pasture where the fissured crags of Cratcliff stand amidst birch woods. Use the right-corner rustic stile and investigate ahead-right for the Hermit's Cave. Protected by metal bars, you can still see the roughly hewn crucifixion and the adjoining rock niche where an oil lamp was kept lit as a vigil by the hermit. The site is thought to date from the 1300s. The main track you followed to reach here is the course of an ancient highway known as the Portway, believed to be a prehistoric route across the hills and moors. The Cratcliff hermit is likely to have acted as a guide for travellers passing here in medieval times. A web of paths criss-crosses the outcrops, but be very aware of the sheer drops here.

Return to the high stile back onto the Limestone Way; turn right a few paces then left over a stile into the walled acreage enclosing the twin-pillared buttress of Robin Hood's Stride. Explore this open access feature at your leisure; it's a bit of a scramble to the very tops. The walk continues by putting the pinnacles on your left as you first approached. Remain within the walled enclosure and work anticlockwise around its edge to the corner with a metal field gate (into a pasture, right) and nearby waymarked stile. Turn right within the woodland edge (woods on your left) to the nearby lane.

3. Turn left to walk over the brow, past the drive to Cliff Farm (right) and then another 400m. Just before a left bend, look carefully for the stone gap-stile and small handgate on your left (there's a fingerpost on your right). Join the descending field path and bear right with it, crossing several pastures via handgates and gap-stiles, essentially heading for the cottages of Elton on the skyline. You'll reach the village edge beside a house's garage; bear right on the access lane here to reach the churchyard at Elton.

4. You join the main street opposite the Duke of York pub. Turn left a few paces; then left on the path before the school. This skirts the right-hand edge of the churchyard to reach a rough track. Look opposite for the continuing path between houses, through a handgate and onwards across a meadow. It's a well-walked path towards a railed enclosure below the steep-roofed cricket pavilion. Slip left of this, up a few steps and through a gap-stile before continuing across sloping pastures. The walked path very gradually loses height and drops away from the line of overhead wires. Within 500m you'll see the corrugated iron roof of a small barn; the path reaches tarred Dudwood Lane just above this. Turn downhill here. Immediately past the second cottage on the right, turn into the parking area, where a footpath sign indicates the handgate and field path across to the main road beyond a strand of trees.

5. Cross straight over, through the little handgate and then over a slab-bridge before climbing the pasture to the top-left corner. Slip left of the barn to join a part-slabbed track, continuing gently uphill for 150m to reach a path junction immediately before two stone gateposts at the edge of woodland. Turn back-right here along the wood-fringe path. Beyond a handgate the way presently passes a tumbled building, then rises below woods, soon skirting the garden at Rocking Stone Farm. Go straight across the waymarked path junction and keep the wall to your left for 150m before reaching a wooded corner. Pass left here, putting the trees on your right, and walk the field path close to the boundary of the woodland. A string of handgates leads into a farm track which emerges on Birchover Lane at Uppertown.

6. This was the original settlement at Birchover. Turn left a few paces; then go right along the rough walled lane, opposite the old village stocks. This winds past first a farm and then a close of cottages. In another 200m look for the signed path on the left. Keep the hedge/fence on your left and advance 600m to reach the complex at Barn Farm. The onward path is right of the stone bungalow; then left up into the right-hand farmyard area. Drift right up the marked path, fence-side beside a camping field on your left, rising easily to a lane. Turn right to a pull-in on the left in 250m, with a National Trust plaque for Stanton Moor Edge.

7. Take the path here and rise, soon beside a fence, to a path junction and information board. Keep the fence on your left, walking the sandy path along the fringe of Stanton Moor, with some great views down the deep valley of the River Derwent. In 1km the Reform, or Earl Grey, Tower is reached. This was erected to commemorate the great Reform Act of 1832, which extended the vote to many more people. Use the stile here and turn right on the wider path, which leads directly to the Neolithic Nine Ladies stone circle.

8. Legend has it that the Nine Ladies and the nearby King Stone were dancing maidens and a fiddle player, turned to stone for dancing on the Sabbath. Depart the circle to pass directly by the King Stone. The path widens and bends left. At a grassy fork in 200m keep left. The track shortly leaves the birch woods and passes well right of the triangulation pillar to reach the pedestal rock of the Cork Stone. Turn right to reach a kissing gate leading to a lane.

Turn left to reach the car park serving Birchover Quarry here. Turn right into it, looking for the path from its rear that turns left along the strip of woodland. Keep ahead over any cross-paths to reach a bend in the road opposite The Druid Inn. Turn left back into the village.

ALONG THE PENNINE BRIDLEWAY TO FABULOUS VIEWPOINTS,
RARELY VISITED CRAGS AND INTRIGUING STONES WAY OUT
WEST.

The final flourish of the Peak District's moors and vales in the west is a jigsaw of ridges, secluded valleys, hamlets and lines of crags familiar to only the most discerning ramblers. This really is the quiet corner of the Dark Peak; criss-crossed by countless packhorse trails, old quarry roads and moorland intake tracks but only recently coming to the attention of casual ramblers with the development of the Pennine Bridleway National Trail, finally completed in 2012. This alternative to the renowned Pennine Way stretches from the southern tip of the Peak District at Middleton to the top of the Yorkshire Dales near Kirkby Stephen.

This airy walk joins the route above the secluded hamlet of Rowarth. The pretty terraces here housed workers who were employed in a string of modest spinning and candlewick mills that were powered by several lively becks. These had closed by the 1930s, although one remains as the Little Mill Inn, overshadowed by a vast, slender waterwheel that was rescued from a nearby mill destroyed in a flood.

The walk strikes along the flank of the Sett Valley, long a popular destination for weekend trippers who flocked here in the 1930s, before rising to summit Lantern Pike. This modest hill gains its name as the site of an Armada Beacon. As such it could be seen from miles around; mirroring this, the views can be impressive, particularly to the nearby Kinder Plateau and along the edge of these southern Pennine moors.

Peaceful farm roads and moorland paths then meander to old quarries which have pitted the scarp of Cown Edge Rocks, before crossing the very edge of the Peak District at Coombes Rocks. The aspect of these inland cliffs is astounding; there's nothing to interrupt the vast views westwards across to Wales, the West Pennines, West Lancashire Hills and the Mersey's course to distant Liverpool Bay. Much nibbled at by quarrying in past centuries, these pillars, crags and cliffs are home to a good range of wild birds.

Towards the end of the walk is the curiosity of Robin Hood's Picking Rods. These two mismatched stone pillars are slotted into a huge base of gritstone. Their purpose is unproven, although they may have acted as a waymarker on an ancient track used by monks travelling between monastic farms scattered amidst the hills. Their connection with Robin Hood is as mysterious as the stones themselves.

THE BASICS

Distance: 8 miles / 12.9km

Gradient: Undulating, with several steady climbs

Severity: Moderate

Approx. time to walk: 4½ hours

Stiles: Many stiles and handgates

Map: OS Explorer OL1 (The Peak District: Dark Peak Area)

Path description: Moorland, field and farm tracks and paths, tarred lanes

Start Point: Rowarth hamlet (GR SK 012892)

Parking: Car park signed from minor roads north of New Mills (free) (SK22 1EF)

Dog friendly: Only suitable for agile and fit dogs

Public toilets: None

Nearest refreshment: Little Mill Inn, Rowarth

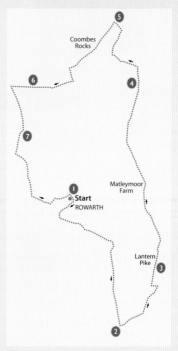

The Route

1. Leave the car park by turning right to the nearby hamlet of Rowarth. At the junction in 150m turn right down the lane, shortly reaching a red telephone box. Fork right on the signed bridleway, a fenced path which slides past secluded houses and cottages and is rather uneven. It presently widens to a track, passing further cottages to reach a junction above the Little Mill Inn. Note the old railway carriage set into the garden; just one quirk of this engaging rural pub.

   The way is left, past the pub and up the tarred lane. Where this forks, keep right to reach Laneside Farm. The route now passes left of this building, declining to a steep, slabby, rough old packhorse trail that climbs towards the moorlands. When it breaks free of its sunken character, some fine views are revealed of the deep little valleys which home in on Rowarth before the water flows south to the River Sett. Our walk also heads south, presently starting a gentle descent as a walled farm lane with some tremendous vistas ahead to the rounded summits and moorland domes above Chapel-en-le-Frith and Whaley Bridge. Keep ahead past any joining tracks, presently passing Wethercotes Farm to reach a T-junction.

2. Turn left down the minor road. Off to your right is the deep valley of the River Sett, channelling waters from the vast moorlands of Kinder Scout down to the River Goyt and, eventually, the Mersey. The large millpond and a few remaining mills recall much busier days in this little valley; at its height in Victorian days several thousand were employed in a string of spinning, printing and paper mills between Hayfield and New Mills.

In 450m you'll reach a short terrace of cottages on the left. Immediately past this, turn left up the tarred lane, signed as the Pennine Bridleway (PB) for Lantern Pike. This rises steadily, eventually passing a secluded house on your left. Beyond this the lane declines to a track and reaches a gateway into the National Trust's

High Peak Estate. Go through this gate and turn left on the rough path up beside the wall. This crests in 150m, at which point (marked by a small concrete post) turn right on the more forgiving path up to the nearby summit of Lantern Pike. The toposcope indicator here names many of the features to be seen on this superb 360-degree panorama.

3. Pick up the well-walked path past the indicator, descending the gentle northern snout of the hill to reach a bridlegate. Keep ahead from this on the braided path, soon merging with a wider rutted track along which bear left to reach the multi-gated corner. Pass through to join the lane, bearing left along this which is again the PB.
Advance to the trees bounding Matleymoor Farm; jink left with the continuing walled track and remain with it for another 600m to reach a second gate across the route. Here the PB bends left; our route is through the handgate on the right, joining a dirt path across the flank of Matley Moor. This reaches a head-on junction with a tarred lane beside a group of horsebox stables. Walk straight ahead on the lane, once again the PB, to reach a T-junction in 550m.

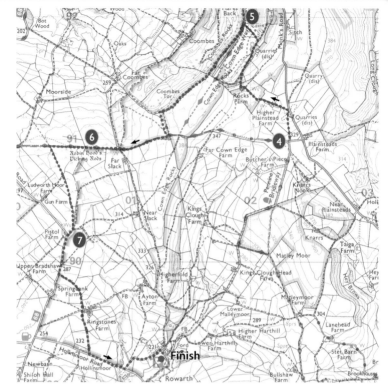

4. Opposite-right is a waymarked stile; climb this into the haymeadow and walk up beside the wall. Where this bends left, keep ahead-right up the pasture, heading for another high stile close to the right-hand telegraph pole on the skyline. From this turn left along the farm road leading to Higher Plainstead Farm. Favour the right fork to pass by the complex of  buildings; then continue on the track to Rocks Farm. Walk into the courtyard right of the farmhouse, where a path is waymarked to the right up past a log store. Use the nearby stile and angle right up the path to a corner marked by a huge tumbled stone.

Bear right here on the path above the broken wall and line of telephone wires. In 120m the distinct path gradually drifts left away from these linear features, rising through the old quarries and low crags of Cown Edge Rocks. When you reach a corner marked by a gate and stile, ignore these and pass left of them on the old track through the workings. This soon crests the ridge and advances to a nearby rickety handgate and stile, with a stand of trees off to your right and another strand to your left.

5. Turn left off the stile, joining the worn path near to the edge of the long line of cliffs and crags that constitute Coombes Rocks. This is the very edge of the gritstone ridges and moors marking the western extreme of the Dark Peak. Below you is a huge embayment of old quarries and workings now grassed over, dappled by ponds. Beyond is an exceptional panorama across the whole of the Greater Manchester conurbation to the West Pennines, along the flats of the Mersey Valley and across Cheshire to the smudge of the mountains of North Wales.

Remain aware of the sheer drops to your right, where jackdaws and ravens abound, sticking beside the path outside the fenced fir woods. Beyond a stile the woods peel away and reedy moorland stretches behind the bounding wall/ fence. Stay true to the edge path for another 600m, when it bends right and the fence turns left. Here, turn left close to the fence and climb the nearby rickety stile. Stay beside the wall on your left; in 150m use a handgate into a gravelled path and walk ahead on this, which turns right and continues as a fenced, firm-surfaced way to reach a gateway some distance to the right of a farmhouse. Now keep ahead on the wider field-edge track to reach the enigmatic stumpy pillars that are Robin Hood's Picking Rods.

6. The field-side track continues beyond this spot. In another 300m is a fingerposted ladder-stile on your left. Use this and head half-left across the reedy moorland pasture to reach two field-gates at a junction of fencelines. Climb the wooden stile here and then aim ahead-right for the far corner-end of the wall on your right. There's a stone-step stile at this kinked corner; use this and then walk ahead, heading just left of the distant farmhouse. A step-stile gains a rough lane here; turn right to the nearby tarred road.

7. Turn left along the lane. In around 350m you'll reach a walled track on your left, signed as a restricted byway. Turn along this to reach the buildings at Ringstones Farm. Look for the tarred lane here, heading to the right away from the complex. At the T-junction in 400m turn left; at the next junction in another 400m turn left for Rowarth to return to the car park.

FANTASTIC TWISTING LIMESTONE GORGES, AIRY PASTURES AND AN ANCIENT VILLAGE IN STAFFORDSHIRE.

The limestone core of the White Peak presents a most complex landscape. It ripples from horizon to horizon as a disjointed jumble of modestly sized pastures, dappled with lumpy knolls, cut by sharp-sided valleys and interlaced by ridges. The most notable landforms are a number of astonishing gorges cleaved into the undulating plateau by a series of swift-flowing rivers which, curiously, you may find flowing vigorously at some times of year, but totally absent at other times.

A string of upland villages have developed on the plateau over the past millennium or so, whilst vestiges of a far older way of life add spice to the mix. Compact Wetton nestles in the lee of one of the most prominent knolls in the area, Wetton Hill. This, and adjoining summits, are capped by the scant remains of tumuli, the burial mounds of Bronze and Iron Age inhabitants who sought a living across these high lands thousands of years ago. Wetton itself probably developed as some sort of centre in the Dark Ages after the Romans departed, but records are lacking. The church is around 700 years old, largely rebuilt in the 1820s.

Close to the village, industrial activity included lead mining at Bincliffe which lasted until the 1880s and the remarkable Ecton Copper Mine a couple of miles to the north, which was the world's richest mine in Georgian times. Copper ore mined here was transported along packhorse trails, some of which we follow, to furnaces at Oakamoor, deeper in Staffordshire, where the resulting metal was drawn into cables that carried the first transatlantic telegraph messages in the 1850s. The landowning Dukes of Devonshire invested some of the profits to develop Buxton as a spa town.

This walk leaves the pretty village via old lanes and paths to pass Thor's Cave, an immense cavern hanging high above the River Manifold, before dropping to the bottom of the gorge. The line of a long-gone narrow gauge railway is followed through marvellous ash woods clothing the Hamps Valley, before a stiff climb achieves the breezy tops at Throwley, with marvellous views the reward. The ruins of a medieval mansion hint at past glories here; the route then drops easily down to the foot of Beeston Tor, a massive crag of limestone renowned among climbers. A final climb regains the edge of the village, where a great traditional pub awaits your custom!

THE BASICS

Distance: 7½ miles / 12km

Gradient: Several steep climbs and descents, otherwise level or gently undulating; many steps down

Severity: Moderate

Approx. time to walk: 4 hours

Stiles: About 10, plus handgates

Map: OS Explorer OL24 (The Peak District: White Peak Area)

Path description: Field and farm tracks and paths, tarred lanes, stepping stones, muddy in places

Start Point: Wetton (GR SK 108552)

Parking: Carr Lane car park (free) (DE6 2AF)

Dog friendly: Only suitable for agile and fit dogs

Public toilets: At start

Nearest refreshment: Royal Oak Inn, Wetton; seasonal café on route

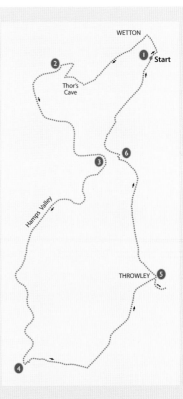

37

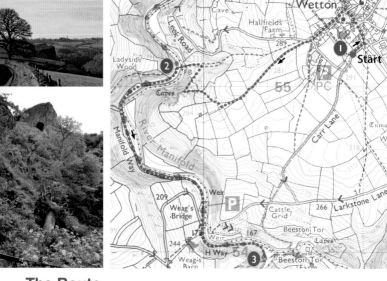

The Route

1. Initially; seek out The Royal Oak Inn opposite the diminutive village green. Head uphill, signed Wetton Mill and Butterton; and bend left, striding past the community hall to the junction at the village edge. Bear right for Wetton Mill; in 50m slip left into the walled track, a concessionary route to Thor's Cave. This wildflower-rich route cuts between meadows to reach a gate-side stile. Enter the small walled enclosure and leave by the waymarked stile at the far-right corner along a field-head path (past a trough) that skirts around the top of a deep side valley. Head for the handgate off the far slope that accesses the path, half-right, leading to the gaping maw of Thor's Cave.

One of the most spectacular cave-mouths in England; its researched history goes back to the last ice age 12,000 years ago. Neolithic stone tools and amber beads have been excavated from its interior, as have the bones of long-extinct animals like cave bears. The fossils of sea creatures add interest; it also featured as a location in Ken Russell's cult 1980s film *The Lair of the White Worm*, loosely based on a horror story by Dracula's creator Bram Stoker. Beware – the cave floor is extremely slippery even in dry weather. The view up the Manifold's twisting valley is exceptional.

Now head down the long flight of steps, keeping left with the sign for Ladyside at a junction. The steep descent ends at a footbridge across the River Manifold. In winter there may be a good flow of water; but after dry periods, and commonly in summer, you'll find no water here. Instead the river's course is marked by a sinuous carpet of the huge leaves of the butterbur plant, growing from the rocky riverbed. The river is still there, but flows underground in a system of fissures; the limestone rock is extremely porous and quickly drains away any water in all but the wettest seasons. The river finally reappears at turbulent springs in the grounds of Ilam Park, some miles to the south.

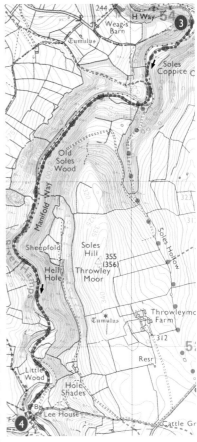

2. Once across the bridge, turn left on the tarred cycleway. This is the latest incarnation of a recreational route that was created as long ago as 1937 by a far-seeing Staffordshire County Council, which spent £6,000 creating the first National Pedestrian Path. It follows the route of the short-lived Leek and Manifold Valley Light Railway, which existed only from 1904 to 1934. At just 2ft 6ins gauge, the small-scale engines were originally built for use on a railway outside Mumbai in India, but instead ended up hauling Edwardian tourists in opulent canary yellow carriages through these spectacular wooded gorges in deepest Staffordshire. The main traffic on the railway was milk from a dairy higher up the valley, taken to the standard-gauge (4ft 8½ins) railway station at nearby Waterhouses from where it was sent to locations across the Midlands.

The route passes through a car-parking area at Weags Bridge, then straight over the minor road and along the right-hand of two lanes ahead. In time these parallel ways part beside a caravan ground. The old wooden building in the field here is one of the few remaining railway buildings. It adjoined Beeston Tor Station, acting as a refreshment room for visitors who flocked here on the eccentric little line in the 1920s.

3. Bending right, the way is now up the gorge of the River Hamps, which joins with the Manifold near the building. The thick, hanging woods here are amongst the finest ash woods in Britain; in spring and early summer the wildflowers are magnificent and the amount of butterfly and birdlife is extraordinary. Walk the ghost of the old railway for 2.5km (1½ miles), crossing a series of flat bridges over the Hamps which, like the Manifold, only flows in wetter months. It's a popular cycleway with family groups, so keep an ear cocked for bells and yells along the way.

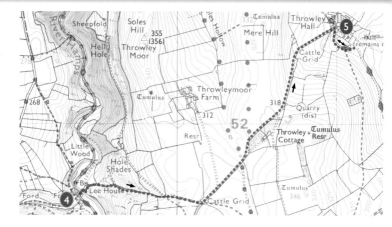

4. Lee House Farm, the only building you'll see in this part of the valley, appears on your left just beyond a bridge. Pass by its driveway and cross another flat bridge. In 50m look left for the footbridge and a path towards the farm. Pass immediately right of the cottage's garden, then bend right to join the steep wood-

edge path (don't use the gates) up the narrow side valley. This can be muddy and slippery in places. Keep uphill in the fringe of the trees to reach a meadow; then ahead over a couple of stiles to reach a tarred lane. Turn left, cross the cattle grid and follow Farwall Lane for 1km (half a mile) to reach the complex at Throwley Hall, indulging all the while in superb views across the White Peak.

Follow the lane to the right through the gated farmyard and round the bend for 400m to view the ruins of Throwley Old Hall. Information boards outline the history of this substantial old towered house, which commands a wonderful prospect down the valley of the Manifold from its lofty perch at the heart of an Elizabethan deer park.

5. Return through the farmyard and turn right at the big circular walled pond, putting this on your left. Bend left around it to a handgate into the clump of trees. Use this and a second nearby; then head up the slight dip in the huge pasture, aiming for the right corner of the strand of woodland on the skyline. You'll join a field road to reach a handgate beside these trees.

Once through, walk to the far edge of the trees and then keep directly ahead down the pasture. On your left are the remains of cultivation terraces – strip lynchets – created in medieval times, best seen lit by a low sun and looking back from the barns below.

At the far-left field corner another handgate leads onto a field road. Breeze down this, passing semi-decrepit barns and noting the sheer cliff of Beeston Tor ahead. The old track bends left above the farm and levels beside the Manifold. Within 100m look for the waymarked handgate, right, to stepping stones across the river. *(If the stones are underwater, then simply continue along the farm road which returns to Weags Bridge. Cross it and walk the lane up to the second cattle grid, then refer to last two sentences below.)*

The cliff face is fractured by huge gashes, one of which hides St Bertram's Cave. This Dark Ages King of Mercia is said to have become a hermit and lived here for a time. The Beeston Tor Cave hoard was found here in 1924, consisting of Anglo Saxon brooches and coins that date the hoard to AD 875.

6.   Turn left off the stones; use the nearby stile/handgate into the National Trust's land and walk ahead 50m before turning left, as signed, up a steadily rising grassy path. Turn right from the gate to reach a minor road. Cross the cattle grid and take the marked field path, left, rising to another lane. Turn up this and remain with it to Wetton, a further 1km.

THROUGH A BRONZE AGE LANDSCAPE TO MEMORIALS AND MEMORABLE GRITSTONE EDGES.

The River Derwent has sliced like a cheese-wire into the land surface in the east of the National Park, exploiting a geological junction between the limestones and gritstones at the heart of the memorable landscapes that characterise this part of the Peak District. This walk sticks to the gritstone, encountering wild moorland and crimped edges offering delectable views to all points of the compass.

Commencing from a country pub, woodland paths and a steep pitch reach the first gritstone edge and a memorial to a military hero before striking out to meander along a shallow moorland ridge. The pillar is one of two memorials encountered along the way. The wild and lonely Big Moor is home to a herd of red deer which may well be seen at any time of year; most easily during the period of the rut, which is during October and early November. Well over 100 animals inhabit the great swathe of moorland tops here; around 3,000 acres are managed as a nature reserve by the National Trust and the RSPB. The moors are important for species such as curlew, wheatear, ring ouzels and whinchats as well as birds of prey like hobbies, peregrines and merlins.

The huge swathe of moorland hasn't always been the reedy waste it appears today. Wind the clock back around 4,000 years and the uplands would have been home to communities of Bronze Age forefathers. Areas were cleared for basic arable farming, with the cleared stones being crafted into simple walls or piled as cairns and mounds, with some created into stone circles. Some of these are passed along the route of the walk, although most are indistinguishable to all but expert eyes. In more contemporary times the moors were used as a training ground for home-guard activities and gunnery training during the last century.

Dropping to join a lower path beside a well-known moorland-edge pub, the route then dips into bluebell woods before emerging onto an undulating path along some of the Peak District's most renowned gritstone edges. Both Froggatt and Curbar Edges have long been popular destinations for ramblers from nearby Sheffield, whilst the rock pinnacles and chimneys, challenging pitches and bouldering opportunities attract a dedicated crowd of adventurers.

Near the end of the walk, another military memorial is encountered before a tranquil stretch through vibrant oak woods preludes the final descent back to the start.

(NB: check Access Land closure information – see p.2)

THE BASICS

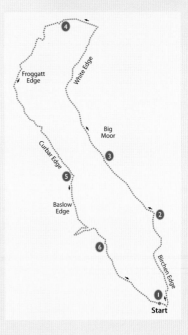

Distance: 9½ miles / 15.3km

Gradient: Gently undulating, several short, gradual climbs, one very short steep rocky pitch near start

Severity: Moderate

Approx. time to walk: 5½ to 6 hours

Stiles: At least 3 plus handgates

Map: OS Explorer OL24 (The Peak District: White Peak Area)

Path description: Woodland and moorland paths, tarred roads, boggy stretches

Start Point: Robin Hood Inn, Chesterfield Road, Baslow (GR SK 280721)

Parking: Birchen Edge NT/RSPB car park beside B6050 road next to pub (fee payable) (DE45 1PQ)

Dog friendly: Only suitable for agile and fit dogs

Public toilets: None

Nearest refreshment: Robin Hood Inn at start; Grouse Inn at halfway point (opening hours vary)

The Route

1. From the car park entrance, turn left and walk past the B & B. Immediately; fork left up the short track by a stone post to a handgate into Access Land. Climb the steps, left, and advance above the B & B grounds. In 200m is a fork beside a large rock. Turn right and tackle the short, steep climb up onto Birchen Edge. It's a well-worn, uneven path up natural steps and boulders. Upon reaching the manhole cover in 100m, turn left and stay with the path above the developing line of crags.

    In 700m you'll reach three distinctive rocks known as the Three Ships. These are dedicated to vessels under the direction of Nelson at the Battle of Trafalgar in 1805 – *Victory* (his flagship), *Defiance* and *Royal Soverin* (that's how it's spelt), named after the first ships to clash with the French fleet at Trafalgar. A few steps further along the path is the slender pillar of Nelson's Monument. Erected in 1810 to celebrate the life of Nelson, who died from wounds at Trafalgar, it was paid for by local benefactor John Brightman.

    Put this on your left and walk the path along the edge of the crags to reach the white-painted triangulation pillar. Remain with the level path, which curls right to clip across a corner of thick heather moor. In around 400m the path bends easily left down through the sparse birch woods before advancing across reedy mossland. It may be boggy in places here, but persevere. The way is largely obvious, although the path does become indistinct in a few places. Your target is the crossroads in the distance, identified by a selection of road signs.

2. Cross into the minor road for Curbar. In 150m take the handgate on your right into access land and pick up the walked path half-left across the moorland, rising gently to a walled corner and fingerpost in 1.5km (1 mile). These upland pastures, separated by partly ruinous walls, have been farmed for four millennia.

3. Take the path signed for White Edge past these ancient enclosures, gradually peeling up away from the wall. Remain on the main path along the shallow edge – *don't* head for the triangulation pillar to your right. Keep ahead another 700m to reach a set of large rocks, where the path bends right and continues along the rim of White Edge, the fringe of Big Moor. Way off to your right are the distant cooling towers of the Trent Valley power stations; a world away.

To your left is the division between the gritstone Dark Peak and limestone White Peak, revealed by the limestone quarries you can spot above distant Stoney Middleton and the deep wooded dales which curl away to the west. Be alert for deer around here; you may spot an antlered head peering from the bracken; or look down to the left for tell-tale furrowed paths made through the high moor-grass and bracken.

Remain on the well-walked path for another 1km (¾ mile), passing one of the Companion Stones, a modern series of a dozen or so inscribed marker stones across the eastern moors reflecting the stoop, or waymarker, stones of earlier times. Eventually you'll reach the lonely crag of Hurkling Stones and, just afterwards, the line of a broken wall. The way is left, down the wall-side path signed for the Grouse Inn. It's a good trod, occasionally rough underfoot as it falls to and through a strand of birch. Use the gate at the far side (it can be very wet here) and cross the intervening rough pasture to reach The Grouse Inn, where ramblers are made welcome (plus dogs and kids in the rear room).

4. Immediately left of the pub's car park use a waymarked stile. Strike through the flower meadows to two closely adjoining stiles that give access to the top of Hay Wood. Turn left immediately within the trees and walk to the nearby NT car park. From the far end of this, a path falls to a step-across of a brook before rising again to a handgate onto the main road.

    Cross carefully, heading right for the nearby white gate and adjoining handgate. The path from here climbs very gently into the woods skirting the top end of Froggatt Edge. When you pass through the next handgate, count out about 200 paces then look left for a lone standing stone just off the path. This is the most obvious member of a small stone circle, the rest of which is under bracken and matted turf here.

    It's now a matter of staying with the wide path along the edge of the moors, marked by the sturdy crags, cliffs and boulder fields that form first Froggatt Edge, then Curbar Edge. It's a popular area with rock climbers, whose sudden appearance over the edge can be disconcerting! Superb views are a given; a grand sweep across the central limestone and gritstone heart, with the great mansion at Chatsworth glowing in the Derwent Valley off to the south. Be aware that there are sheer drops for the next 3km. The path, firm and obvious, eventually passes through another handgate; keep right to the nearby lane and cross to the continuing path opposite via another handgate.

5. Advance along Baslow Edge to find the isolated Eagle Stone in 750m. Allegedly this enormous block was climbed as a test of strength and agility by local men wishing to prove themselves worthy to a sweetheart. Select the lesser path angling half-left to Wellington's Monument; inconspicuous against the trees. This was conceived both to celebrate the Iron Duke's victory over Napoleon's forces at the Battle of Waterloo in 1815 and to 'balance' the memorial to Nelson, passed earlier in the walk. It was commissioned in 1866 by a local bigwig, Dr Lieutenant Colonel E.M. Wrench.

    Turn right from the monument (woods on your left) and remain on the widening path for 400m to reach a stubby walled corner and gate. Turn back-left on the lesser path immediately above the wall/fence. For 300m this is through high summer bracken; it then descends gently (uneven in places) through the oakwoods. Beyond a narrow, enclosed section of path after a handgate, cross the stone bridge high over Bar Brook and continue to the road opposite a cottage.

6   Look left for the step-stile into a woodland path. Take this and curl behind the house on a gently rising woodland path that presently passes above a tumble-walled field. Advance gradually uphill across the brackeny slope, with views across Baslow, then through the tongue of woods below the stone tors of Gardom's Edge. Beyond an open gateway the path then strikes gradually downhill well right of Moorside Farm, a grassy trod presently reaching the main road. Turn left to the nearby pub and car park.

PAST A HIGHWAYMAN'S LAST STAND TO A STRING OF INCREDIBLE CANYONS AMIDST CARPETS OF MARVELLOUS SPRING WILDFLOWERS.

The valley of the Derbyshire River Wye is one of the most familiar and popular areas to visit in the entire National Park. At its heart is Bakewell, often thrumming with visitors ambling its lanes and ginnels before dispersing to pretty villages such as Ashford-in-the-Water or palatial houses like Chatsworth or Haddon Hall. The valley also has a string of renowned scenic highlights, some of which are more easily accessible than others, and surprising industrial heritage tucked away deep in wooded vales hidden until you stumble into them.

This walk makes the most of such diversity, starting from one of the most famous panoramic viewpoints before meandering off the beaten track to discover unvisited, sublime acres of the White Peak and plunging into the most delectable of limestone gorges. Monsal Head's viewpoint has wowed visitors since Victorian days. The magnificent vista of the deep, twisting gorge of the Wye as it swirls through thick woodland blanketing precipitous hillsides features in a million postcards. Its artificial focal point, the bold, arched viaduct across a bend in the river, improves the experience for some whilst attracting condemnation from others, notably the Victorian commentator John Ruskin.

Our walk leaves this setting to pass through pretty Little Longstone; then weaves along old byways through long-abandoned and reclaimed quarrying and mining areas to gain open country near Wardlow Hay Cop, a secluded top with some grand views. Adjacent to this is the immense chasm of Cressbrook Dale; a path curls along the lip of this fabulously wildflower-rich gorge before descending into the depths and cool ashwoods of the National Nature Reserve.

Small settlements such as Cressbrook and Litton Mill lie tucked away here. They owe their existence to textile mills built in the Wye Valley to take advantage of the water to provide power and washing facilities to process cloth. Litton Mill, now an idyllic backwater, had the worst of reputations for using child labour in the darkest days of Victorian England. Between these hamlets is Water-cum-Jolly Dale, a simply astonishing millpond that has flooded the Wye's gorge. Our path strikes through the gorge below towering cliffs and bluffs beside this hidden gem; after which a path scurries up the valley side to gain the Monsal Trail. This old railway is followed past idyllic Upperdale onto the striking Headstone Viaduct, a suitable finale to a beautiful walk.

(NB: check Access Land closure information – see p.2)

THE BASICS

Distance: 8¼ miles / 13.3km

Gradient: Undulating, with several steady climbs and one steep descent

Severity: Moderate

Approx. time to walk: 5 hours

Stiles: About 6, plus many handgates; 2 gap-stiles at Point 2 are very narrow

Map: OS Explorer OL24 (The Peak District: White Peak Area)

Path description: Moorland, field, woodland and farm tracks and paths, tarred lanes, old railway

Start Point: Monsal Head (GR SK 185715)

Parking: Pay and display car park or limited roadside parking (DE45 1NL)

Dog friendly: Only suitable for agile and fit dogs

Public toilets: At start

Nearest refreshment: Pubs at and near start; café at start/end

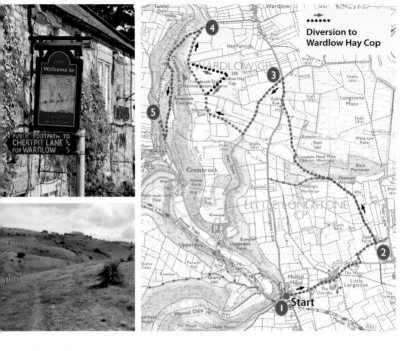

The Route

1. From the Monsal Head Inn take the lane directly opposite for Little and Great Longstone. Little Longstone is soon reached; pass the Pack Horse Inn and continue through the village, little more than a strand of cottages beside the lane. Just past the last house on the left, look for the waymarked, walled path up alongside the driveway to 'Longstone Byre'. Follow this waymarked path via handgates around the rear of the grounds and along the pasture edge to reach Dale Farm.

2. Turn left up the old walled track, rising gradually between pastures. In 1km it reaches sparse woods and levels just beyond a bench. Look right, off-track, for the stile leaving a walled enclave into a rising field road, which passes above a dew pond and through grassy workings of the former Crossdale Head Mine. This was one of the larger mining concerns here at Longstone Moor. It reached a depth of 350 feet (100m) and worked until the 1870s, with galena (lead ore) the main product.

   At the wall, turn right with it 20 paces; then look carefully for the concrete-step stile on your left opposite trees. Cross this and bear right, continuing on the higher field track angling gradually away from the wall. As this crests look ahead-left for a small handgate, beyond which aim 60m above (right of) the left-hand clump of trees, and use the narrow gap-stile and then another in the next fence above the roadside pens. Use a further stile then head to a gap-stile onto the road. Turn right to the crossroads in 250m.

3.   Turn left down the lane, remaining on this for nearly 1km (¾ mile) to reach, on your right, a field track and a nearby waymarked handgate by an information board about Cressbrook Dale. Walk the grassy field path up the shallow valley and bear left alongside the cross-wall. Use the handgate and advance to the corner. A waymark points right; head for the gate halfway along the far wall. Pass through this. The way is ahead on the continuing grassy track through scrubby pasture across Access Land. You can divert to the summit trig point of Wardlow Hay Cop to your right, a 400m diversion each way; views from the top can be extravagant. Local tradition has it that here, in the mid 1700s, a notorious highwayman named Black Harry was captured by sheriffs and constables from Castleton and later hanged on the gallows tree at nearby Wardlow Mires.

You need eventually to end up at the top-left corner (as you entered it) of the scrubby pasture, where a handgate finds a path at the fringe of a precipitous drop into Cressbrook Dale. Turn right beside the wall and tread the walked path for around 400m to reach a path junction by the wall corner.

4.   Turn back-left on the path which soon drops steeply down into woodland that clothes the impressive dale. Go left at the hill-foot, and in a while cross the little wooden footbridge and turn immediately left on the path just above the stream. This strikes through these wildflower-rich woods, presently  reaching a gate into a lane at Ravensdale Cottages, a picturesque fold of cottages associated with the local cotton mills. Simply remain with this as it climbs easily to a junction. Cross diagonally onto the path rising through the woods to reach another lane; turn right to the junction and here go left into the hamlet of Cressbrook.

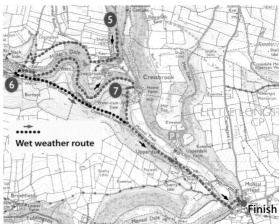

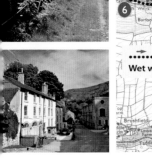

5. Head up the rising lane past terraces of stone-built cottages and the village club. Pass by a lane joining from the left, soon reaching St John's Church. Immediately past the cottages here, fork left on the walled track signed for Litton Mill and Millers Dale. This loses height increasingly steeply as it falls towards the valley. Keep ahead where the track issues into pasture, tracing the green field track down to S-bends beside the old chimney, which is the flue from former lead smelters in the valley below. Drop down the narrow valley into the hamlet of Litton Mill.

6. The glorious setting of the stone mill, now apartments, belies the wretched time that was had by workers there – in particular child labourers – in the decades after the mill was built in the 1780s. Established by local landowners, its name became synonymous with the worst excesses of exploitation in the textile industry. It used the waters of the Wye to turn waterwheels, then turbines, to generate power.

NB. In very wet periods the next riverside section will be impassable. In this case, at Litton Mill turn right 30 paces from the red phone box; then go left on the path beside the sewage pumping station. Cross the footbridge and head up the path up to the Monsal Trail. Go left, following the old railway through two tunnels all the way back to Headstone Viaduct. Then see last sentence of the walk.

Pass between the gates and down past the mill complex here. From the far end a well-signed path crosses the mill-race before maturing as a good track beside the River Wye (to your right). The wooded gorge sides of Miller's Dale presently peel apart a little, at which point the top

of the millpond that fills Water-cum-Jolly-Dale is reached. It's a magnificent walk alongside this hidden waterscape, eventually reaching a path junction just over a footbridge at the dam and weir.

Just downstream from here is another impressive building, Cressbrook Mill. Again, it was established as a cotton mill, this time by the famous industrialist Richard Arkwright in 1779. Hundreds of people eventually worked here, nominally at least treated better than those at Litton Mill. Orphans brought up from London were accommodated in apprentice houses here, whilst the housing in Cressbrook village passed earlier in the walk was provided for families. A major product was fine cotton, used in the lace industry in Nottingham. The mill eventually ran out of steam in 1965 and was then used as a stone-cutting works for many years before being turned into apartments.

7. Cross the second footbridge directly over the weir and climb the path up through the woods. This bends left up steps and levels as a ledged path, presently reaching the route of the old railway near a tunnel entrance. This was the Midland Railway's main line between Manchester and London, built at huge expense in the 1860s. It closed in 1968 and remained a mysterious linear ruin until much of it was reopened in 1981 as a multi-user recreational trail, The Monsal Trail. It was only in 2011 that the tunnels on the line were restored to use on what is one of the most scenic railway trails in the country.

Turn away from the portal of Cressbrook Tunnel and walk this lovely elevated trail, with some great views down into the Wye Valley, to reach the Headstone Viaduct. Cross this, then fork left up the steep path before the tunnel mouth, which rises back to the Monsal Head Inn.

WALK THE FRINGE OF THE NATIONAL PARK IN SUPERB, TRANQUIL MOORLAND COUNTRY ABOVE THE TAME VALLEY.

The slender pillar on the Pots & Pans will be familiar to many rail travellers on the Huddersfield to Manchester line. It's the War Memorial to the servicemen of Saddleworth's villages. A bracing walk up from the Tame Valley to the ridge gradually unveils a phenomenal series of views across the South and West Pennines known to only a select few ramblers; a secluded, private panorama across the roof of England. The memorial is sited amongst crags and outcrops of extraordinarily weathered gritstone. The Pots & Pans stone is just south of the memorial. In certain lights it's said to have bumps and hollows that resemble a human face. Folklore has it that druids practised here, and that waters taken from the various hollows can help cure eye infections.

The way strikes north along a dip below the ridge-top, with wonderful views taking the eye to the north and west. Dropping from the heights to the gaggle of houses, cottages and inns at Saddleworth Fold, there's chance to sample microbrewery beers at The Church Inn and find the fascinating 'Bill o' Jacks' memorial stone in the spooky, overgrown churchyard here. This commemorates an unsolved murder that gripped the attention of the populace nationwide in 1832. The landlord and son at a remote moorland pub, The Moorcock Inn (now long gone), were savagely murdered. The press frenzy that ensued ensured that as many as 2,000 people attended the funeral of the victims. The walk then strikes north again, crossing reedy pastures and beside an old leat to reach lanes heading for Diglea, one of the oldest and most attractive hamlets in the area.

Beyond here the long and short routes diverge. The shorter version picks up the towpath of the Huddersfield Narrow Canal beside the southern portal of Britain's longest, highest and deepest canal tunnel, the 3¼-mile (5.2km) long Standedge

Tunnel. A long series of locks drop the towpath and canal gradually down into the Upper Tame Valley, eventually reaching the car park where the walk started.

The longer route climbs up to the long ridge of Harrop Edge to join the original pre-turnpike road between Yorkshire and Lancashire. This leads to Dobcross village centre; a picture-perfect South Pennine stone village. The Swan Inn here is where the Wrigley family, members of which emigrated to the USA and founded the renowned chewing-gum company, were tenants in the 18th century.

THE BASICS

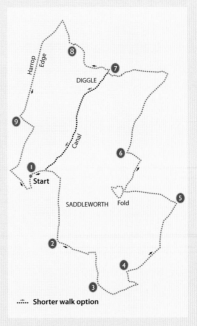

Distance: 6 miles / 9.7km or 8¼ miles / 13.3km

Gradient: Undulating, several steady climbs

Severity: Moderate

Approx. time to walk: 3½ or 4½ hours

Stiles: About 10, plus handgates

Map: OS Explorer OL1 (The Peak District: Dark Peak Area)

Path description: Field and moorland paths and tracks, tarred lanes, old railway, towpath

Start Point: Brownhill, Uppermill (GR SD 996065)

Parking: Wool Road car park, off A670 220m north of Brownhill Countryside Centre [free] (OL3 5QR)

Dog friendly: Only suitable for agile and fit dogs. On leads near main roads

Public toilets: Brownhill Countryside Centre

Nearest refreshment: Several pubs on route; Limekiln café at Brownhill

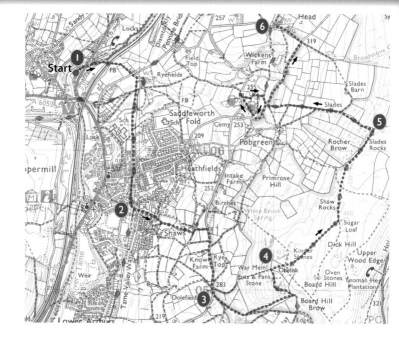

The Route

1. From the car park entrance cross to the cobbled cul-de-sac and bus turning area opposite-left and join the rough lane rising between cottages numbers 18 and 20. Branch ahead off the nearby sharp-right bend, cross the railway footbridge and ascend the fenced path, then pasture, to meet a lane just to the right of the farm buildings. Slip left a few paces; then go right at the junction on the tarred lane, also the Pennine Bridleway. In 30m turn right down the waymarked sandy path to join the route of an old railway. Cross a cross-track and continue ahead another 375m to reach a fork beside a fenced hard-play area; here keep ahead-left. Cross the first wooden footbridge above a road and continue to cross a second 275m later.

2. Here; turn back-left down the path to the nearby lane and turn up this, Station Road. At the junction with Grove Road in 75m keep left up Shaws Lane. At the higher junction by a grit box keep left. The way roughens, becomes cobbled then rises to a T-junction. Turn left; in 40m turn right up the sunken track, climbing to a tarred lane at 'Rowans'. Turn right and walk for 450m to the point it starts descending steeply next to a stone house.

3. Here, fork left on the rough track (not the footpath) off the top of Haw Clough Lane. In 50m keep left at the fork, rising to use a gate. Pass below wires; then in another 100m nudge left off the sunken track and up the distinct grassy path rising across the snout of the hill. It meets a wider path below an area of tumbled stones; turn left to work up to the War Memorial pillar here at Pots & Pans.

It's dedicated to all Saddleworth's war dead, Saddleworth being the collective name of half-a-dozen gritstone villages peppered in and above the Tame Valley hereabouts. The Pots & Pans stone itself is the tor-like lump of rock before reaching the obelisk.

4. As you approach the pillar, look half-right for the gap in the old iron-rail fence; marked by an 'Oldham Way' (OW) stone. Keep ahead from this, passing just right of the stony outcrop in 75m to find a gate-side stile (OW) which leads into a moorland track. Trace this through the wide, low depression between the low ridges, rising then to a point before the track

crests, about 600m. Turn left here on a defined grassy path which passes the distinct, rounded Sugar Loaf stone to reach the bristly outcrop of Shaw Rocks. Advance past these on the good path; cross the stile then remain beside the fence line ahead. The way soon comes alongside an old wall; keep ahead to find a decrepit fingerpost in a reedy dip just before the next stile.

5. Go left here (OW), dropping beside the broken wall/fence with the decrepit barn well off to your right beyond rough pasture. At the field gate go ahead on the right-hand track to a corner. Here slip ahead over the stile, then drop beside the scrappy wall down to a lane. Turn left to find the Cross Keys pub in 175m. The Oldham Mountain Rescue Team is based here. From the back corner of the car park a waymarked path drops one field to The Church Inn and Saddleworth parish church. Look for the Bill o' Jacks grave in the back-left corner of the graveyard behind the old hearse house here. Then take the path up beside the church (with the old stocks on your left), which slides up past a farmhouse, continuing up the driveway to the lane. Turn left. At the crossways in 600m go left, steeply downhill to reach the houses at Running Hill Head.

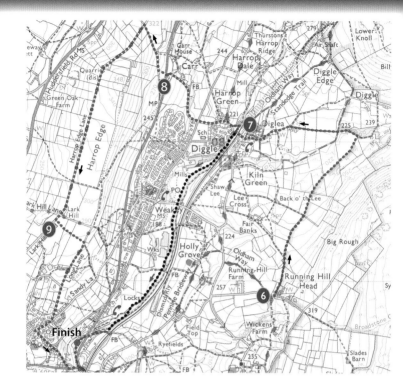

6. As the lane levels here, look right for the narrow, enclosed path immediately before Running Hill Farmhouse. Walk with this over two stiles to a walled corner and trackside pylon. Slip right here, putting a wall on your right. Swap sides at the next stile, remaining wall-side. Shortly, cross a  walled track, then keep ahead to the offset walled corner. Use the gap-stile here; then another stile at the corner ahead. Advance in-line just right of the visible distant arched bridge. A marshy section brings you to a reedy leat; turn right alongside this, keeping it on your right to eventually reach a tarred lane a little way downhill from a mill complex now redeveloped as housing. Turn left to reach Diglea village and cross the railway bridge beyond the Diggle Hotel.

7. *For the shorter walk*, turn left off the bridge to the nearby corner and Sam Lane car park. From the rear of this join the canal towpath at the southern portal of the Standedge Tunnel and simply follow this all the way back to the car park, swapping sides of the canal at Lock 25W.

   For the longer walk, turn right off the bridge and walk 50 paces to find the footpath, left, up beside houses. At the top turn right to the nearby tree-studded little green at Harrop Green. Bear left on the lane, continuing through the hamlet to reach the main road. Cross into narrow Carr Lane and follow this all the way through, eventually rising steeply to the main A62 road beside a house.

8. Turn right to find a rough track on the left in 50m. Join this; soon bend hard-right with it and continue uphill to the crossways on the ridge beside a fir-tree plantation. Turn left along the rough, wide track, rising more gently along Harrop Edge Lane. This old packhorse way offers some great views into the deep valley of the River Tame around Delph to your right, as well as a grand prospect across Saddleworth. In 1.5km (1 mile) you'll reach the secluded grit-stone farmhouse at Lark Hill.

9. Turn left here on another walled track. At the sharp bend in 200m turn right to follow the continuing track which, at a terrace of cottages, becomes tarred. Keep ahead to the junction above bungalows in 350m; here bear right to walk in to the centre of Dobcross. Film buffs may recognise The Square here as a location in the 1979 Richard Gere film *Yanks*.

Turn left past The Swan pub and walk the 150m to the bend. Here, slip ahead-right along the narrow Nicker Brow, which steepens past cottages as a wide, surfaced path into the Tame Valley. Emerging beside an old stone-built mill, head left to the mini-roundabout. Circle right, into the yard in front of Brownhill Countryside Centre. Drop to the towpath and turn right, passing under the bridge to find the car park in 200m.

POIGNANT TALES AND MAGNIFICENT MOORLANDS ABOVE THE GREAT RIFT OF LONGDENDALE.

Around 12,000 years ago a vast ice-sheet scoured out a colossal trough that almost completely breaches the line of The Pennines. Longdendale is one of the deepest and most shapely valleys of the South Pennines. This great slice through the line of hills is also one of the main transport corridors across England's watershed. The Woodhead Pass carries countless vehicles between the north-west and Yorkshire; until the 1980s an electric railway also burrowed beneath the moors here. This is now the Longdendale Trail recreational route, part of the Trans-Pennine Trail linking Southport and Hull. This walk uses a stretch of this before escaping to the high moorlands north of the pass; a truly wild area just a short hop from Manchester's urban fringe.

It's a remote, secluded countryside, where mysteries tantalise and a tragic heritage haunts the peaty groughs and deep cloughs. None more so than the strange lights that are regularly seen. The 'Longdendale Lights' are an unexplained phenomenon that illuminate the valley and dance across the heights of Bleaklow, Black Hill and Kinder. Wills-o'-the-wisp, aircraft headlights, ball lightning and police helicopters are amongst the explanations offered, but the mystery remains. Spookily, countless aircraft have crashed on the vast moors here over the years, with usually fatal consequences.

The walk first visits the small Woodhead Chapel above the hamlet of Crowden, where unmarked graves recall tragic accidents during the construction of the railway and bring to mind the 28 victims of cholera which swept through the reservoir navvies' camps in 1849. The way then drops to pick up the converted trackbed of the Manchester to Sheffield line, first opened in 1845. At much the same time, construction of a string of vast reservoirs was commenced, damming the River Etherow to supply water to Manchester's burgeoning population and the needs of the textile industry of the conurbation.

Skirting these, our route then climbs an old quarry track which threads through birch and fir woods. The walk then grips the rim of the great plateau of Black Hill, passing crags and waterfalls which serrate this great natural wall. Keep an eye out here for mountain hares, which in winter develop white fur to disguise them from the predatory falcons and foxes which hunt these snowy upland margins. The return to Crowden crosses the mouth of the spectacular Crowden Great Brook, one of Peakland's hidden scenic gems.

(NB: check Access Land closure information – see p.2)

THE BASICS

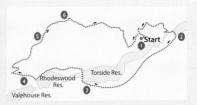

Distance: 8 miles / 12.9km

Gradient: Undulating, with several steady climbs

Severity: Moderate

Approx. time to walk: 4½ hours

Stiles: Sixteen stiles and handgates

Map: OS Explorer OL1 (The Peak District: Dark Peak Area)

Path description: Moorland roads and paths which can be uneven and boggy, surfaced tracks and tarred lanes

Start Point: Crowden (GR SK 072993)

Parking: Peak Park car park at Crowden (free) (SK13 1HZ)

Dog friendly: Only suitable for agile and fit dogs. On leads near main roads.

Public toilets: None

Nearest refreshment: Bulls Head Inn, Tintwistle is 3 miles (5km) west, off the A628

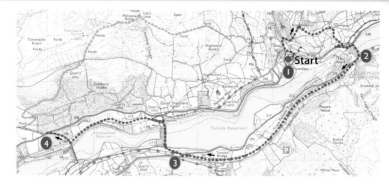

The Route

1. From the car park entrance turn left; then left again, signed Outdoor Education Centre. At the crossways in 100m turn right towards the Centre, large barns on your left. In 50m fork right up the rougher field road, which curls right (ladder-stile) to reach a sharp-left bend. Look for the stile off the upper part of this bend; a steep path climbs right of the outermost tree to level close to another stile. Turn right off this to pick up the nearby moorland track and walk this, the old quarry up on your left. This was Loft End Quarry, much stone from which went for use as kerbstones in Sheffield and

Manchester. Follow this track across the hillside for 650m to a junction with a cobbled track. Turn downhill, meeting the tarred lane to the compact St James' Church – Woodhead Chapel – beside the boundary wall. Despite the proximity of the main road, it's an atmospheric spot. A church has stood here for 550 years.

Descend the access lane to the busy main road. Cross carefully and turn left on the thin pavement. Opposite the driveway to Bleak House, use the steps behind the handgate and drop down to the road across the dam of Woodhead Reservoir. Building commenced on this, the highest of the string of five reservoirs, in 1847 but took 30 years to complete, the last to be finished. At the height of construction, over 1,000 people worked on the vast Manchester Corporation Waterworks Company scheme. The designer was John Frederick Bateman, one of the greatest of Victorian civil engineers.

At the far side slip left into the car park to reach the Longdendale Trail multi-user route. This is the line of the old main line between Manchester and Sheffield; one of the earliest of the cross-Pennine railways, it opened in stages from 1845. Way off to your left, beyond the head of Woodhead Reservoir, three tunnels penetrate the gritstone hills. The first opened in 1845; the last in 1954, when the route became the first main line in Britain to be electrified. At over 3 miles (5km) in length, they're some of the longest in the country. Sadly, passenger services were discontinued in 1970, and the final freight train passed through in 1981. A narrow-gauge inspection railway was then installed, used to access the high-voltage electricity cables which now thread below the moors through the newest tunnel – the cables that you pass below at the car park.

2. Turn right on the old trackbed and simply follow this compact-surfaced track (signed Trans-Pennine Trail for Torside) for nearly 2 miles (3km). Gaps in the tree cover reveal fine views, right, across Torside Reservoir to the precipitous valley sides, crags and moors the walk is destined for. Closer to hand, a number of adventurous paths head up steep side cloughs climbing towards the huge expanse of Bleaklow on your left.

3. Cross the road where the Pennine Way is met. Bear right a few paces, then left on the descending wide track (still Pennine Way) to and across Torside Dam. At the far side bend left to reach the sharp-right hairpin above the house. Slip through the gap by the lower gate, then climb to the higher track above the trees fringing Rhodeswood Reservoir. This is the route of the former reservoir railway system, built to a narrow 3-foot gauge. It was initially worked by steam locomotives, but in 1904 it was converted to use electric engines, the power generated from one of the dams until 1950. The whole system was dismantled in the late 1960s.

As you reach Rhodeswood Dam, take the lane up to the right to the main road. Rather than supplying water to Manchester, Valehouse Reservoir, below you, and Bottoms, the last in the line, were built to act as feeders to the River Etherow, assuring a constant head of water down the river to the many mills further down the valley. This was a condition of the scheme going ahead; as it was, a number of very large mills once stood where the waters of the reservoirs now glisten. Above Rhodeswood Reservoir stood the shanty town of New Yarmouth, where the labourers who created the reservoir dams and waterworks lived in appalling conditions in wooden and turf hovels. This is where cholera struck.

4. Cross diagonally over the busy A628, joining the signed Restricted Byway which rises steadily beyond the gate. In 200m bend sharp-right, then ignore two branches to the right, and instead zigzag to a higher gate-side stile (with an Access Land disc) into the woodland. Use this; the continuing track climbs steadily through these mixed woods, presently passing above the first of many boulder-strewn slopes marking old quarries. Views are enchanting: steep slopes richly dressed with heather, bilberry and occasional yew; fir and birch woodlands; the string of reservoirs in Longdendale far below and the endless mass of moors forming Bleaklow and Kinder beyond. The wide track ends at old workings that echo with the sound of waterfalls tumbling over the upper edges from the high mosslands. Keep ahead on the thin path which climbs steadily (awkward underfoot) past final workings to reach a stile onto the open moors.

5. Turn right over the stile, step over the beck and ahead another 10 paces, then turn left along a well-defined moorland path, often marshy in places (if you reach the ladder-stile over the moor-edge fence you've gone just too far). The endless expanse of rolling moorland, split by deep groughs, holds a tragic secret. Over the past 70 years

a considerable number of aircraft have crashed onto the moors and into the low ridges and tops which constitute Black Hill. Foul weather, faulty navigation, pilot error, low cloud and instrument malfunction are just a few theories as to why so many aircraft have been lost. At a few locations there are considerable remains to be seen, but those nearest to this spot (Lancaster Bomber PA411  lost in December 1948 plus a number of Hurricane fighters and an American P38 Lightning) are fiendishly difficult to find amidst the deeply eroded moors.

The path drifts gradually right towards the crags of Millstone Rocks, then clips the lip of the steep scarp before curling left to Lad's Leap, a gash cut into the edge.

6. Cross the head of this; turn right to pass the large cairn and strike ahead to reach the stretch of fallen wall. Angle left here along the distinct hollow in the moor for 200m before drifting right beside the continuing old wall. Pass through another derelict wall; soon after this head down to the isolated little stand of trees well above the pale-stone Outdoor Education Centre. Views from this section up the chasm of Crowden Great Brook are sublime.

At the wood-edge memorial to Harry Phillips, turn right through the handgate along the Pennine Way. Upon reaching the tarred lane go left, presently passing a campsite, located on the site of Crowden Hall, built in 1692 and demolished in 1937. At the crossways by the huge barns, keep ahead, then turn twice right to return to Crowden car park.

ALONG ASTONISHING WOODED DALES AND TOWERING GORGES IN THE WHITE PEAK HIGH ABOVE BAKEWELL.

The limestone plateau of the White Peak is liberally seared by deep gorges, commonly named as dales. The most spectacular of these circumscribe a generous arc to the north, west and south of Bakewell, where the River Wye and its labyrinthine family of tributaries have scoured canyons both large and small into the uplands. This walk winds along a series of these delectable dales, varying in scale from a spectacular National Nature Reserve to half-hidden dry valleys, wooded gulches and craggy corners.

The route starts from a plateau car park close to calcite workings that still provide materials to the chemical and pharmaceutical industries. Initially following the waymarked long-distance Limestone Way, the walk drops steeply into Bradford Dale, a beautiful wooded valley watered by a crystal-clear stream, before passing through one of the area's prettiest villages, Youlgreave. Heritage and a fine church detain the visitor before the way advances to start a wonderful ramble up one of the finest limestone dales in the country, Lathkill Dale.

Countless weirs create both sparkling waterfalls and deep, limpid pools in the gently winding valley. A wealth of birds make their home here; look in particular for the white-bibbed dippers, kingfishers and wagtails whilst there's a similarly generous variety of butterflies to take the eye throughout spring to autumn. Limestone-loving plants are one of the main reasons that the dale is a nature reserve; rarities include the bright blue Jacob's Ladder, which is the county plant of Derbyshire.

Hidden in the Dale are sturdy remains of the lead-mining industry that flourished here for centuries. Much is disguised or overgrown; but those at the Mandale Mine are easily seen on a short path from the riverside. The thick woodlands peel back to reveal the spectacular landscape of a limestone gorge at its best. In summer the river here is flowing well underground, leaving a sinuous course of butterbur plants to fill the riverbed. In winter waters gush from springs and side valleys such as Cales Dale, meaning that the walk has a different character every season.

Cosy Fern Dale is the escape from the main valley; after this an airy route across the plateau is interrupted only by a steep in-and-out crossing of Cales Dale.

THE BASICS

Distance: 9 miles / 14.5km

Gradient: Undulating, with one very steep, long flight of steps up

Severity: Moderate

Approx. time to walk: 5 hours

Stiles: Many stiles and handgates

Map: OS Explorer OL24 (The Peak District: White Peak Area)

Path description: Field and riverside paths and tracks, tarred lanes; some later paths are rough underfoot

NB The path in Lathkill Dale is closed each Wednesday between November and January inclusive. Don't attempt this walk on these days.

Start Point: Moor Lane, Youlgreave (GR SK 194645)

Parking: Peak National Park car park (free) at Moor Lane or nearby lay-by (free) (near DE45 1LU)

Dog friendly: Only suitable for agile and fit dogs

Public toilets: Youlgreave

Nearest refreshment: Pubs and tearooms in Youlgreave

The Route

1. Join the gated cart track alongside the car park. In under 100m keep straight ahead, ignoring the fork to a barn. Beyond a handgate the path drops diagonally across a falling meadow, passing long-forgotten grassy delvings which dapple the slope. The way peels left down to a small handgate into a lane. Turn left on this; immediately round the nearby bend look for the waymarked Limestone Way (LW) on the right, down steep steps. The path passes through a strand of sycamores; then downhill to a gate into a tarred road; here bear right along the pavement. The imposing house secluded behind the wall is Lomberdale Hall, once home to Thomas Bateman, a renowned Victorian archaeologist and antiquarian who first investigated many of the archaeological sites that dot today's Peak District.

    In 300m the road bends sharply left. Immediately after this bend, slip left onto the continuing LW, falling now down a deeply cut wooded dell. This twists around to the floor of the larger Bradford Dale; cross the River Bradford on a sturdy bridge. Upstream is a low dam; our way is left and downstream, passing the first of a long series of pools created to manage the fishing. It's a delightful stroll at any time of year, particularly in late spring with a flurry of wildflowers to appreciate.

2. The path reaches a clapper bridge, above which the cottages of Youlgreave ascend steeply beside tranquil paths and lanes. Cross the bridge (leaving the LW) and walk up the lane to emerge at the main village road. Turn right, shortly passing the imposing old cooperative store – now a Youth Hostel – and the unusual circular stone tank that once was the village water supply. Passing the Bull's Head and then

the village pie shop, the road reaches a crossways beside the imposing All Saints Church. Take time to visit this ancient building; inside are fine medieval tombs, old carvings and some widely admired stained-glass windows by the renowned Arts and Crafts designer Edward Burne-Jones.

Turn left at the crossways, putting The George Inn to your right. In around 250m fork right down the narrow 'No Through Road' immediately past the village telephone exchange. Winding between haymeadows this presently drops to pass by secluded Raper Lodge. The way is now left along the track above the spinney; a short diversion ahead down the path reaches a lovely spot beside the River Lathkill where a bridge spans a weir. This area featured in the 1970 film adaptation of D.H. Lawrence's *The Virgin and The Gypsy* starring Franco Nero and Joanna Shimkus.

3. Having turned left on the track, remain with it as it narrows to a path, advancing then to reach a lane. Turn right to reach and cross the squat, solid Conksbury Bridge. In 1941 a Wellington bomber from 149 Squadron crashed close by in the thickly wooded dale, having run out of fuel whilst returning from an air raid over Bremen. The crew had already baled out and survived. Once across the bridge turn upstream on the signed footpath and keep to the riverside, soon passing the first of a long line of pools impounding the Lathkill's turbulent course. In 1km the route reaches the old mill and house below Over Haddon.

4. Don't cross the clapper footbridge here. Instead; jink right 15m, then left to pass beside the steep-roofed mill on a wide and firm path which continues up thickly wooded Lathkill Dale National Nature Reserve. Just beyond a gate, a side path deviates the short distance to the gaunt remains of the Cornish beam-engine house at Mandale Mine. Exploration off the path isn't recommended as there are hidden pits and holes. Return to the main path and continue upstream, Past a couple of gates the trees peel away on your right, revealing the nature of this fabulous dale as a great limestone gorge. The derelict weir nearby marks the site of Carter's Mill, recalled by old millstones in the bank. Further weirs disturb the passage of the waters before the woods eventually draw back from the southern flank of the gorge too. In very short measure a footbridge crosses the river near old mossy walls.

    Again, don't cross this bridge, which leads to a path up the cleft of Cales Dale. Instead remain in the main valley along the now much rougher path. In a very short distance is the summer source of the river, where the waters bubble out of a hidden source in the hill-foot just behind the wall. In wetter periods the source is reached some 700m further upstream, where the great dark maw of Lathkill Head Cave is wreathed in shadow on your left at a point opposite another lesser side-dale. The Lathkill springs from the cave during much of the winter.

Staying with the main path ahead, it presently becomes more challenging underfoot as the gorge sides close in. A fenced area on the left is there to protect the rare Jacob's Ladder flower from grazing sheep over the summer months. Beyond a squeeze-stile are a number of rockfalls marking the various workings of the long-closed Ricklow Quarry. The limestone rock is particularly rich in fossil crinoids, or sea fans; this became very popular as a 'black marble' building stone in Victorian days. Scant remains of an old tramroad climb to the heights above; our route continues to climb the shallowing gorge.

5. Beyond a handgate the gorge dissipates. At this point look left for a walled and gated field track entrance with a step-stile. Don't use this; instead slip up the narrow dale behind. It's a good path up the shallow valley of Fern Dale. Several stiles and gates bring you to the top of the dale, where the path curls right to reach a National Trust sign, a handgate and an LW fingerpost. Use the gate and turn left along the LW to a further handgate, beyond which keep the wall on your immediate left. A string of handgates and stiles leads to One Ash Grange Farm, approaching this on a rough walled lane.

6. Pass immediately right of the first stone barn, then bear left on the path signed for Lathkill Dale and LW. Passing an unusual pigsty and then a shrine contained in a stony alcove, the waymarked way heads between iron-clad and stone barns, shortly dropping down natural limestone steps and below an overhang before reaching the bottom of Cales Dale. Here; climb the stile and start up the long, steep steps on the path for Calling Low and Youlgreave. After the handgate at the lip of Cales Dale the path is a well-walked route across upland pastures. Several handgates take the continuing LW through the strand of trees to the left of Calling Low Farm, then onwards to pass through the left-hand corner of the wooded Low Moor Plantation ahead. Once through the trees and back in pastures, pick up the continuing path through a series of stiles and gates to reach a lane at a junction and lay-by. Take the diagonally opposite lane back to the car park in 150m.

To the roof of Cheshire and a remote valley wreathed in mystery.

An engaging walk in the quietest, most remote and little-known corner of Cheshire leaves from a ridge-top car park that offers delectable views across the splintered gritstone ridges and deep vales of East Cheshire and also a great panorama of the corrugated fringe of the Dark Peak. Starting at this height means that it's an easy, gradual gain of height over the first 3km. The first sub-summit on the ridge is Cats Tor. Off to the east, hidden below the plantations of conifers, is the deep valley of the River Goyt. Partly filled by the reservoirs of Errwood and Fernilee, which supply Stockport, it was home to a gunpowder factory for over 300 years; it supplied powder for Drake's fleet against the Spanish Armada in 1588 and kept on producing until after the Great War, eventually closing in the 1920s.

The views only get better as the walk reaches Shining Tor, the highest point in Cheshire (559m/1,834ft) and a popular area for hang-gliders and paragliders. The panorama is suitably extensive, with waves of rounded tops and moors interspersed by glimpses of craggy gritstone outcrops. A clear day reveals the Clwydian Hills to the west, the West Pennines to the north and The Wrekin and Long Mynd way down south in Shropshire. More immediately, the buildings near the masts on the near eastern horizon are the Cat and Fiddle Inn, the second-highest pub in England. Remarkably, this edge of the Peak District has four of the country's highest pubs.

Turning back from Shining Tor, the route drops into the atmospheric valley of Thursbitch. Researchers and experts have identified a series of ancient standing stones incorporated into walls or fallen and hidden in the moorland grasses; its history is long and wreathed in legend. The renowned author Alan Garner wrote a novel (*Thursbitch*) about the area. It's a somewhat disquieting fiction-based-on-fact/folklore tale about this secluded place, the name of which is derived from the Old English for 'Demon Valley'.

Passing remote Jenkin Chapel, the walk snakes down Todd Brook Valley between far-flung farms nestled beneath sycamores; ruins recall more prosperous times in this land of haymeadows and reedy pastures. Popping in on tiny Kettleshulme, once a centre for manufacturing candlewicks, the walk then rises steeply to Taxal Edge, with mouth-watering views of Kinder and Brown Knoll's shadowy moors, to skim Windgather Rocks, a favoured training area for crag rats.

THE BASICS

Distance: 10½ miles / 16.9km

Gradient: Undulating, with several steady climbs

Severity: Moderate

Approx. time to walk: 5½ to 6 hours

Stiles: Many stiles and handgates

Map: OS Explorer OL24 (The Peak District: White Peak Area)

Path description: Moorland, field and farm tracks and paths, tarred lanes, marshy in places

Start Point: Pym Chair free car park (GR SJ 995767)

Parking: Pym Chair is along minor roads 4 miles (6.5km) south-west of Whaley Bridge; follow signs for Goyt Valley and Saltersford off the B5470 between Whaley Bridge and Macclesfield (nearest postcode is SK10 5XL)

Dog friendly: Only suitable for agile and fit dogs

Public toilets: None

Nearest refreshment: Swan Inn, Kettleshulme, on the route

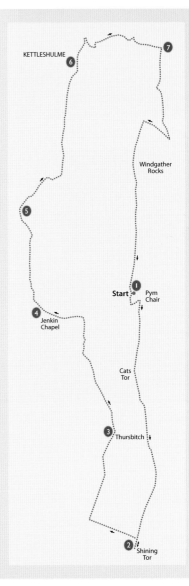

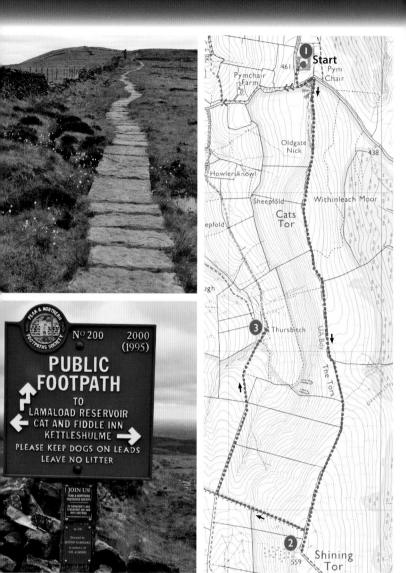

The Route

1. From the car park go left to the nearby T-junction and turn left. The information board here speculates about the origin of the name of this spot on the ridge, Pym Chair; preacher or felon, the choice is yours! At the crest beyond the cattle grid look right for the handgate signed for Shining Tor, picking up the well-defined path along the ridge here. It's simply a matter of walking this fence-side trod for nearly 3km (2 miles). You'll soon drop through the dip of Oldgate Nick before passing the crags of Cats Tor. The route presently becomes a flagstoned path; these slabs are likely to have come from demolished textile mills in the Pennine foothills.

You'll reach the summit of Shining Tor at a walled corner, where the trig pillar is over the wall on your right. Ahead, shapely Shutlingsloe takes the eye; off to the left is the Cat and Fiddle pub whilst the dark scar beyond is The Roaches. The clearest days will allow views to the distant tops of the Clee Hills near the Shropshire/Herefordshire border and the mountains of the northern Welsh Marches.

2. Turn back from the summit along the path on which you approached. At the cast-iron 'Peak & Northern Footpaths Society' footpath sign (120m) for Lamaload, cross the step-stile to join a descending wall-side path. At the corner stile in 600m, just beyond the dip, turn right on your side of the fence and remain beside this, dropping into the top of the Todd Brook Valley. At the second subsequent stile, change sides of the wall/fence and follow the field path as it bows across rough pasture to reach twin stiles above a brook. Use the right-hand one and reach the nearby farmstead ruins via another stile. This is Thursbitch; as lonely a site as you'll find hereabouts and long abandoned.

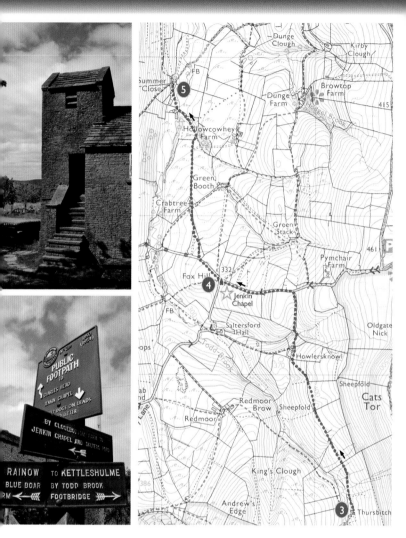

3. From the ruins, join the developing grassy track beyond the two stone gateposts. The old farm track advances across the flank of Cats Tor, coursing above the deepening Todd Brook Valley to your left. Crossing a series of rills cut into the steep slope, several gateways and stiles draw the track to a gate and stile fronting a clump of trees. These shelter Howlers Knowl Farm. Pass immediately right of the trees, use the ladder-stile and drop left to a handgate into a track. Turn right and walk on this up to the tarred road; turn downhill to reach Jenkin Chapel amidst its ruff of trees. This cute construction dates from 1733, built for a local landowner and used by both the scattered local community and by jaggers (packmen) guiding their strings of packhorses along these switchback old saltways that linked the Cheshire saltfields with the growing towns of the north Midlands. If it's unlocked, you can revel in a totally unaltered, rustic period interior.

In the adjoining valley is a remote lane-side memorial stone to a jagger, John Taylor, of nearby Saltersford Hall Farm. He was found frozen to death on Christmas Eve 1735; beside him in the snow, untouched by the hoofmarks of the pack ponies, was the single footprint of a woman's shoe.

4. Head along the 'No Through Road' directly opposite the church. In 170m go right, over the fingerposted stile, then drift left to join a farm road along which head right. Remain on this, a pleasant and easy ramble along firm tracks below the long ridge of Broad Moss. Keep left at the junction over an old cattle grid beside the gaunt ruins of Crabtree Farm; then left again at the fork for Hollowcowhey Farm. The track meanders through a copse before crossing Todd Brook; keep right with the track here and rise gently past barns to approach the secluded farmhouse at Summer Close.

5. Bear right at the gate on the path for 'Kettleshulme by Todd Brook Footbridge'. In 40 paces slip right off the track, down the reedy meadow to cross the visible footbridge. Head half-left off it across an extremely reedy, damp field to a stile near the far  top corner beneath a thorn tree. Beyond this, advance beside the line of gnarled trees; at their end look right for a waymarked stile, beyond which step over the brook and walk up to the abandoned farmhouse.

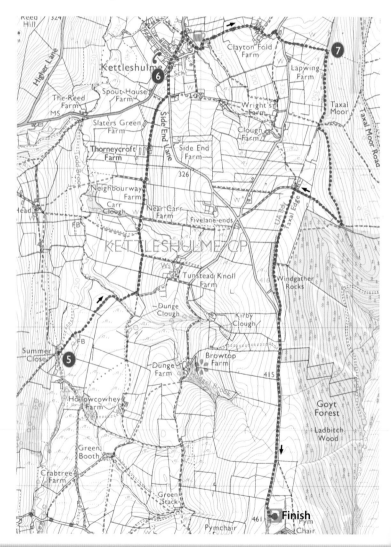

Use the stile immediately left of the building and turn left along the wall-line. Cross two more stiles, then go ahead-left beside the wall to the nearby renovated cottage. Join the rough access track, which later becomes tarred, passing several more properties before reaching a T-junction in 750m. Turn left to Kettleshulme. In Georgian times this secluded village was a centre for silk manufacture (used to produce buttons) in small village mills powered by the waters of the Todd Brook. This declined in early Victorian times, to be replaced by the manufacture of candlewicks; the last wick mill closed in 1937.

6. Turn right down the main road to reach The Swan Inn, in the valley bottom. Cross the road and walk uphill to the nearby bend. Turn back-right on the rougher lane 'Unsuitable for Motors'; at the junction in 200m turn left up the steep, tarred lane. Stick with this, rough in places, past further secluded properties to reach a minor road, just round a left bend in 500m. Turn right, uphill. Just round the bend in 100m use the stile on the left, waymarked for Taxal. Stick by the wall; as it eventually fails, keep ahead up the steepening haymeadow to a handgate on the ridge-top.

7. Turn right through the gate and simply remain on the wall-side path for the next 1km. It undulates along Taxal Edge, skirting the edge of Access Land all the while. Ignore any side paths or tempting gates and keep the wall on your immediate right. This will bring you to a path junction at the edge of firwoods. Here turn right, then fork right in a few paces on the path signed for Backhillgate, walking through a gap-stile and then along the pasture edge and past a lone tree to reach the farmhouse. Turn left in front of the building on the wall-side path signed for Windgather Rocks.

There's a gentle ascent before the escarpment is reached. A grassy path skims the top of the sheer western faces of Windgather, which are frequently busy with climbers, before continuing ahead parallel to the nearby lane. Pass through a gate and keep company with this concessionary path off-road, skirting heathery moorland before rejoining the lane's verge close to the car park.

EXPLORE SOME OF THE CLASSIC LANDSCAPES OF THE WHITE AND DARK PEAKS ABOVE ENGLAND'S CAVE CAPITAL.

'All this country is hollow. Could you strike it with some gigantic hammer it would boom like a drum, or possibly cave in altogether and expose some huge subterranean sea.'

So wrote Sir Arthur Conan Doyle in his 1910 short story 'The Terror of Blue John Gap'. Whilst his tale of monster-hunting in the underworld is engagingly fanciful, his description of the country around Castleton has more than a ring of truth to it. The area where the Dark and White Peaks meet and mingle is riddled with delvings and workings; pot-holes and quarries; fissures and caverns that are the result of a complex geology and the determination of humans to wrest a living from the landscape.

Castleton itself is the focus for a series of four caves and caverns that have proved popular destinations for travellers and tourists for many decades. The little town's hinterland is dappled by gorges and ravines formed by the action of water on limestone. This walk starts up one such; Cave Dale may be the remains of a collapsed cavern, or created by meltwaters from the great ice-sheets of the last ice age scouring through a weakness in the underlying limestone. Either way, this deep, winding gash in the land takes the walk up onto the limestone plateau above. Old quarry tracks and packhorse ways thread through a White Peak landscape of miniature dales, crags and old lead mining remains, skimming above the village of Peak Forest before looping back to the distinctive line of hills that tower above Castleton.

The Great Ridge is pure Dark Peak; gritty sandstones, silts and shales eroded into a ridge of resistant rocks towering over the older limestone dome to the south. This advantage was seized on by Bronze and Iron Age peoples who developed fortifications across the width of today's central Peak District, the most notable of which is the hillfort on Mam Tor. Its spectacular site is enhanced by the landslips that have cut away its eastern ramparts, creating the great curving cliff that is still unstable and suffers from rockfalls.

The walk heads across the top of the Tor and continues to Hollins Cross, from where another of the unstable peaks, Back Tor, is seen. The route then doubles back along an abandoned main road to indulge in a final limestone treat; a descent of the fabulous Winnats Pass to return to Castleton.

THE BASICS

Distance: 8¾ miles / 14km

Gradient: Undulating, with several steady climbs

Severity: Moderate

Approx. time to walk: 4¾ hours

Stiles: Around 30 stiles and gates

Map: OS Explorer OL1 (The Peak District: Dark Peak Area) and OL24 (The Peak District: White Peak Area)

Path description: Tarred lanes, field and farm tracks and paths, dirt roads, boggy in short stretches

Start Point: Castleton village centre (GR SK 149830)

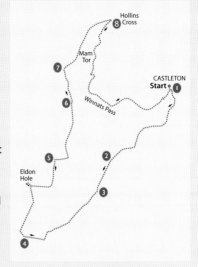

Parking: Main village car park (pay and display), Cross Street (S33 8WN)

Dog friendly: Only suitable for agile and fit dogs. On leads near main roads.

Public toilets: Castleton

Nearest refreshment: Tearooms, pubs and restaurants in Castleton

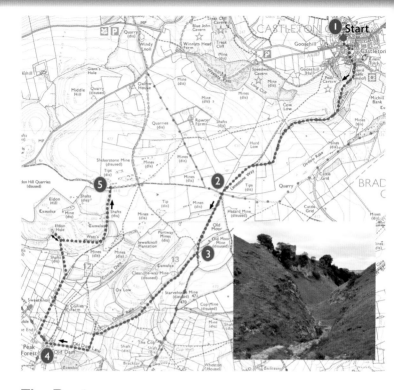

The Route

1. Find The Castle Inn and turn up Castle Street beside it. Peveril Castle has stood on its lofty crag for over 900 years. Built by William Peveril, illegitimate son of William the Conqueror, in about 1080, it acted as a centre for the Royal Forest of The Peak for centuries. Originally a wooden motte and bailey, its commanding stone keep was added by King Henry II in 1176. By the time of Elizabeth I it was largely abandoned, with just the keep kept in use as a courtroom. its sombre appearance adds to the delight of visiting the site – perhaps after this walk!

    Bear left at the top of Castle Street; then slip right of the grassy Market Place, seeking the narrow entrance to Cavedale squeezing right, beside Dale Cottage. Advance up the dale, which opens out slightly below the cliffs and crags that acted as a natural defence for the castle. Today these pinnacles and faces are the haunt of jackdaws. It's a memorable walk up this ravine, with a few sightings of the castle to be had. Looking back, there's a fine view across the rooftops of the village to the distant Great Ridge. The dale's sides gradually diminish and the bridle path breaks free of the crags to become a grassy track up a shallowing valley. Pass through two bridlegates; then keep the wall on your right to reach a gate/stile into a moorland track.

2. The walk continues along the signed bridleway (and Limestone Way) directly opposite, keeping the wall immediately on your right. The undulating plateau of the White Peak unfolds, pockmarked by countless old workings. These were mostly lead mines; the Castleton area was one of the most important lead fields in the country, worked from Roman times until the 1900s.

3. In 600m the pasture thins to a point with several gates. Here turn right on the bridleway (leaving the Limestone Way) between fence and wall, alongside a long set of grassed-over diggings. These follow the line of a vein, or rake, of galena ore from which lead is obtained. This particular one is Oxlow Rake; the nearby Clear-the-Way Mine was over 330ft (100m) deep, it closed over a century ago. With some fabulous views ahead, the track presently passes through a spinney of contorted ancient beech trees. Keep left of the barns to reach a gate onto tarred farm driveway; turn left to the T-junction and right to the hamlet of Old Dam.

4. From the small circular green, bear right along the main road for 150m; then turn right up Eldon Lane. As the tar fails at the higher farm and barns, keep ahead through a gate in 100m then bend left with the wall. Use the gate past the end of the woods; then keep beside the wall to find the bushy entrance to Eldon Hole some 100m beyond another gateway. This was classed as one of the Seven Wonders of The Peak in the 1600s and was greatly admired by the renowned author Daniel Defoe, writer of *Robinson Crusoe*. It's an immense chasm nearly 250 feet (75m) feet deep cleaved into the flank of Eldon Hill, said to be home to elves! Keep well back from the sheer drops.

Return to the nearest gateway; once through it head half-left, past the little limestone exposure and across the hill flank. In 300m bear left along a line of small hollows, another worked-out lead rake. Head up to the clump of trees in the corner; here turn left beside the wall (**not** over the double stile) and accompany this past a metal handgate to reach a moorland track in 600m.

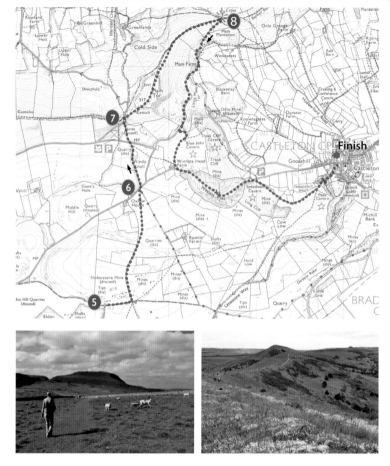

5. Turn right; then in 200m, just through a gate, turn left over a waymarked stile onto the wall-side path and persevere with this through several more gates/stiles. As the wall bends left towards Oxlow House farm, aim for the far-right field corner and a gate onto the main road.

6. Turn right a few paces; then left through the handgate onto a wide field-edge track that heads towards the obvious gap in the ridge ahead. This is Mam Nick; simply walk to this using gates as appropriate and passing straight over another road en route. Until 1979 this was the main A625 road across the Peak District. In that year it was abandoned after the latest of a long history of landslips on the southern face of Mam Tor – the 'Shivering Mountain' – swept the road away.

7. At Mam Nick take the gated, paved path on the right, past the National Trust's Mam Tor sign. The slim top of this ridge is enclosed by the ramparts of a hill fort originating in the Bronze Age over 3,000 years ago. At its height in the Iron Age, perhaps 100 huts stood in the enclosed area, defended by ditches and wooden

palisades. The panorama is exceptional, taking in the lengths of the twin valleys here – the Vale of Edale and the Hope Valley – as well as a great view of the Kinder massif to the north above Edale and the great sweep of the White Peak spreading to the south.

Leaving the summit, remain on the gently descending, paved path to arrive at a major junction of ways at Hollins Cross, at the first dip in 1.3km (just under a mile). Directly ahead, the eye is taken by the sheer face of Back Tor and beyond it the rounded summit of Lose Hill.

8. Our way is sharply back-right, through a handgate and down the path to reach redundant stone gateposts before the woods. Keep above the trees on the occasionally boggy path, which threads across the slope to meet the course of the abandoned road at a sharp bend. Turn up it and walk the shattered road, remaining on it to reach the signed access road to Blue John Cavern. Turn along this. The cavern is renowned for its bands of rare Blue John Stone, and is one of the caves open to the public. The mineral calcium fluorite, stained by hydrocarbons, is still mined here in small quantities during the winter months. Take the grassy path from the handgate to the right of the building as you look at it. This skims across the limestone pasture towards Winnats Head Farm; turn left at the farm boundary wall to a handgate onto the tarred road.

Now; turn downhill and descend the spectacular collapsed cave that is the Winnats Pass. Or is it a glacial meltwater cut? Or a trough cut by turbid currents in an ancient sea? You pays your money… However it was formed it's one of the most memorable landforms in the National Park. Grassy paths skirt the road to reach the mouth of the gorge and the entrance to Speedwell Mine, another of the show caves, this one reached by underground boat.

About 50m below Speedwell, take the path on the right, signed as the National Trust Longcliff property. Simply trace the grassy path above the curving wall, presently emerging beside a house at the top of Castleton. Drop to the bridge over the river and bear left to the centre.

ARTHURIAN LEGEND, FOLKLORE AND COLOSSAL CRAGS HIGH
IN THE STAFFORDSHIRE MOORLANDS.

Climbers have flocked to the memorable bluffs and cliffs of the sudden gritstone edges above the old market town of Leek for decades. The crags are challenging to all grades of mountaineer; leading exponents in British climbing cut their teeth here before tackling some of the planet's toughest ascents. This airy ramble explores the lanes and woods around the memorable outcrops of The Roaches before threading along the spine of the ridge, unlocking some astounding views and encountering age-old tales along the way.

A hill road skirts the edge high above the headwaters of the Meer Brook. Strung along below the exposures of the Five Clouds and The Roaches, views from this centuries-old route stretch deep into the Staffordshire countryside and across to the line of the Gritstone Trail. Tracks and paths then meander to the ridge-end overlooking the deep, sinuous valley of the River Dane, which acts as the boundary between Staffordshire and Cheshire. Looping back into magnificent birch, oak and beech woods smothering the valley slopes, the way threads into the astonishing chasm of Lud's Church, where King Arthur's nephew Sir Gawain is said to have met with the fearsome Green Knight. One of the oldest of folklore tales comes to a head in a spectacularly beautiful and remote part of the Peak District.

Escaping the rather spooky mossy and fern-fronded chasm, the walk presently leaves the trees to reach the gritstone ridge at Roach End. From here the way rises easily past a string of fantastically eroded outcrops of rock given fanciful names like Bearstone. It's a grand, bracing walk along the edge of the moorlands. To one side, beyond a veneer of pine woods, is a patchwork of haymeadows and rich pastureland dappled with dairy farms and cornfields. To the other is wild moorland; a colourful blanket of heather and bilberry-clad slopes sliced by deep cloughs and etched with long lines of crumbling stone walls forming ghostly fields.

Passing an upland pool where a mermaid is said to tempt unwary passers-by to a gruesome end, the walk finally enters an area of sharp crags, cliffs and pinnacles towering high above Tittesworth Reservoir. This is where you'll likely see climbers testing their mettle. Far less confident are creatures almost as fabled as mermaids and Dark Ages heroes; there perhaps still exists a wallaby or two in the thick undergrowth, so keep your eyes peeled!

THE BASICS

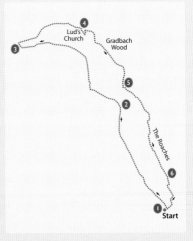

Distance: 7 miles / 11.3km

Gradient: Undulating, with several modest climbs and short steep descents

Severity: Moderate

Approx. time to walk: 4½ hours

Stiles: Five plus several handgates

Map: OS Explorer OL24 (The Peak District: White Peak Area)

Path description: Tarred lanes, field and woodland paths; several sets of steep steps, awkward underfoot in places, expect mud

Start Point: Roaches Lane, Upper Hulme (GR SK 005620)

Parking: Roadside lay-bys 400m past Roaches Tearooms (ST13 8UA)

Dog friendly: Only suitable for agile and fit dogs

Public toilets: None

Nearest refreshment: Roaches Tearooms at Paddock Farm near Upper Hulme; Ye Olde Rock Inn at Upper Hulme

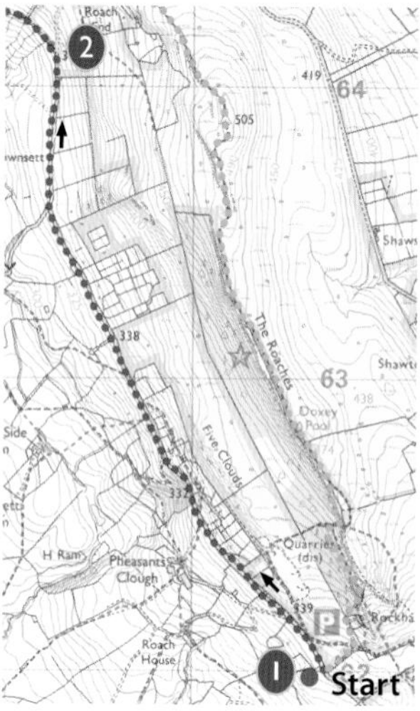

The Route

1. From whichever lay-by you've used, turn along the road and head north, with the rolling expanse of North Staffordshire set out at your feet to your left. The stretch of water is Tittesworth Reservoir, which captures the headwaters of the Meer Brook for the benefit of the people of Leek and the towns of The Potteries further downstream. It was created in the early 1960s, greatly enlarging a lake that was empounded in Victorian times to feed the silk mills of Leek, which demanded large quantities of water to allow complex dyeing to be completed.

   Up to your right are the snouts of a series of distinctive crags. These are the Five Clouds and mark the edge of the lower tier of the parallel ridges that create The Roaches; rough pasture in contrast to the verdant vale below. This has been farmed since medieval times, when the lands were granted to the Abbey of Dieulacres in 1214. The hamlet of Roche Grange in the valley recalls its foundation as a farm serving the needs of the Abbey, which was just to the north of Leek. A grange is a 'daughter' settlement; the 'Roche' is from the French word for rocks, as is the name of the Roaches escarpment. Stay with the lane along the flank of the hill, keeping ahead at the fork and heading for Royal Cottage.

2. About 75m past the gate across the road, and where the wall turns left, branch left along the grassy track. This – occasionally boggy – remains close to the wall on your left, thinning to a path beyond a gate before reaching another surfaced lane. Here go left; then turn right before the nearby cattle grid up the marshy rough field. Bend right beneath the line of telephone wires to rejoin the lane a little higher up and advance along this over another cattle grid. In about 500m, at a left-hand bend, diverge ahead-right on a field path for Back Forest to a use gate-side stile. Turn left for Swythamley and remain beside the wall at the foot

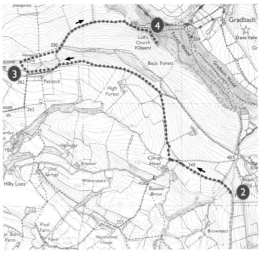

of the steep slope. In just over 1km the path reaches a junction by a gate. Pass through; then walk the concessionary path for Swythamley just above the trees. At the gravelled driveway head right over the cattle grid; then turn immediately right up to the nearby Hanging Stone.

3. This modest snout of gritstone is a long-recognised local landmark. Certainly the Brocklehurst family, who owned The Roaches estate and lived at the substantial Swythamley Hall, visible in the valley below, were taken with it. Two memorials are extant on the rock; one recalls the favourite mastiff of a former master of the house; the other is a memorial to a family member who died in the Second War. It was this latter, Henry Courtney Brocklehurst, who established a private zoo on the estate in the 1930s. During the Second World War, fodder for the animals became impossible to source, so he released some of them to fend for themselves. These included yaks, llamas, emus, an antelope and some Bennett's wallabies. Of these only the wallabies made a go of it. They were regularly seen until the turn of the century, then only rarely, although sightings in 2015 confirm their offspring are still out there. The Hall, now apartments, was in the 1970s and 80s a centre for transcendental meditation, owned by followers of the Maharishi Mahesh Yogi, famous for his association with The Beatles.

Ascend the steps beside the rock, then drift right on the grassy, waymarked concessionary path. This arrows across the moorland high above the remote Upper Dane Valley, allowing some exceptional views across this deeply fractured area of the Peak District to the shapely summit of distant Shutlingsloe. Use a stile-cum-handgate and advance to a cross-wall. Drop down the stile and go left alongside the wall on the sandy path, keeping ahead at the nearby waypost for Lud's Church. Allow the wall to turn away left in 400m; you follow the sunken path ahead to the nearby woods.

About 100m into the trees, fork right at the clearing along the higher path signed for Lud's Church. The entrance to the chasm is easily missed; look for it on your right in a further 150m at some old wooden railings, a thin gap between low cliffs. Steep steps plunge down into the defile. It's wreathed in mystery and intrigue. Sir Gawain, of Round Table fame, met the Green Knight here to discharge a vow in a Dark Ages tale of courtly chivalry and deceit. The Green Knight is said to sleep in the gorge – or green chapel – still. In the 15th century it was a meeting place for religious dissenters called Lollards, organised by Walter de Lud-Auk, who worshipped here in secrecy and great danger. Lud is derived from Walter's surname. The origin of the feature is less prosaic; it's the result of a landslip that fractured the gritstone and left the memorable cleft through the hillside.

4. Steps at the far end lead back out of the depths. Bear right on the path and remain on this through the beautiful broadleaf woodlands, obeying several signs for Gradbach/Roaches. This well-walked path leaves the woods at a grove of huge beeches (signed right for Roaches), rising beside a wall to reach a stile onto the lane at Roach End.

5. The onward path is opposite, signed as the main path to The Roaches. A steady, gentle climb ensues, soon passing by the first of a series of wind-and-water weathered outcrops of rock, The Bearstone. The summit triangulation pillar is reached, after which it's a gently undulating stroll along the rocky ridge. Down to your left is the site of an aircraft crash, where in 1941 a German Junkers Ju 88 bomber plunged into the side of the hill whilst returning from a raid on Liverpool Docks.

    The path hugs the edge of the sheer cliffs, with mouth-watering views along the shapely crags towards Hen Cloud, the final bluff. A curious feature is the little tarn of Doxey Pool. It's rumoured to be the haunt of a beautiful, malevolent water sprite who tempts innocent men to their doom in the pool's depths.

6. Carry on alongside the broken wall on your right until you reach the spot where it ends in a distinct dip. Here's a short, steep path to take, which drops down into the fir woods clothing the middle-level of the escarpment. Turn left just past old wooden rails  and trace the path below the lofty crags, eventually reaching two stone gateposts at the end of another old wall. There's another flight of rock-cut steps down to your right here, from the foot of which it's a short step to the wall surrounding the odd building of Rock Hall. This hobbit-like home was the cave refuge of highwaymen and army deserters, then a gamekeeper's cottage in the 1870s; it's now a climbing hut.

    Work your way down beside the wall and then left to the lower, wider track. Turn right on this to reach the main lane along the foot of The Roaches. Your car awaits, depending where you parked.

TACKLE ELUSIVE PEAK DISTRICT PEAKS ON A CHALLENGING
CIRCUIT IN THE UNFREQUENTED UPPER DOVE VALLEY.

Squirreled away at the top of a valley where Dark Peak and White Peak meet is a string of
shapely limestone hills. Erupting precipitously from the flat floor of the upper Dove Valley,
they rise like gigantic fins from a sea of green. They tower above the north-eastern bank of
the Dove, whilst to the south-west the character of the rock is different; rounder shoulders
of darker gritstone form the edges and moors of the Dark Peak from which the Dove, and
its near-neighbour the River Manifold, spring a few miles away on Axe Edge.

This energetic ramble starts from Longnor. Perched on a ridge, this once prosperous
market centre lost its way in Victorian times when its market trade was taken by larger
towns connected to the developing rail network. A latter-day plan to extend the narrow-
gauge Manifold Valley Light Railway to Longnor from nearby Hulme End came to nought,
and the little Staffordshire town became the pleasing backwater it is today.

A track drops into the valley before paths across Access Land tackle the abrupt hills
on the Derbyshire side of the Dove. These are the remains of reefs formed in tropical
seas 340 million years ago. Their genesis makes them more resistant to erosion than the
surrounding rocks, hence differential weathering has resulted in these striking knolls –
genuine Peak District peaks!

Beyond Glutton Bridge, a steep path first conquers Parkhouse Hill before the roller-
coaster continues to the summit of Chrome Hill's rippling ridge. This is nicknamed the

'Dragon's Back' because of its resemblance, from a distance, to the scaly plates on the back of a stegosaurus dinosaur. The walking is particularly challenging, with two steep climbs and several very short, extremely steep descents that require particular care. The rewards, however, amply repay such diligence.

Tumbling down Chrome Hill's snout, the way then loops round to join a wonderful old salters' trail which drops to a picturesque pack-bridge over the Dove. One of the most secluded and secret parts of the Peak District; it can hardly have changed in centuries.

The route then advances to the attractive hamlet of Hollinsclough. This huddle of cottages, church and chapel was once a thriving silk-weaving location, where farmers supplemented their income as outworkers to larger mills in Leek and Macclesfield. It's a gentle walk on tranquil lanes back towards Longnor.

(NB: check Access Land closure information – see p.2)

THE BASICS

Distance: 7¼ miles / 11.7km

Gradient: Undulating, two sharp climbs and short very steep descents

Severity: Challenging

Approx. time to walk: 4½ to 5 hours

Stiles: Six plus many handgates

Map: OS Explorer OL24 (The Peak District: White Peak Area)

Path description: Field and moorland paths and tracks, tarred lanes, some precipitous drops adjoin

Start Point: Longnor (GR SK 088649)

Parking: Longnor Market Square or on Church Street (free) (SK17 0NT)

Dog friendly: Only suitable for agile and fit dogs

Public toilets: Longnor Square

Nearest refreshment: Tearooms and pubs in Longnor

The Route

1. Face Longnor's eye-catching Market Hall, still bearing its bill of rates, and turn right along High Street, passing Ye Olde Cheshire Cheese pub. At the edge of the village, turn left up the lane named both Top o' th' Edge and Dove Ridge. At the fork by cottages in 150m, bear right through the gateway down a concreted track. This hairpins right at a barn; here slip left to find the continuing path signed around the side of the barn as a bridleway for Beggar's Bridge. It's a well-worn path across pastures, heading directly for a deep gap in the hill-line ahead. Once over the bridge across the River Dove, advance up the wide green track to reach a tarred lane at a corner.

2. Turn left on this. Pass straight through the complex at Underhill and remain on the rougher old lane, presently passing a secluded cottage and then a turn (right) to a farm. Keep faith with the lane to reach a road opposite a garage at Glutton Bridge.

3. Turn left and then go right on the tarred lane just past the telephone box in 100m. Walk this until you cross the cattle grid. Ahead you've got a fine view of the profile of Chrome Hill; but first there's the matter of Parkhouse Hill to conquer. This is now Access Land, so you've a free choice of which is the best route to the top. The line of least resistance is to turn right off the cattle grid and walk to and past the offset wall corner a little way up the field. Once at the top corner, bear right for 30 paces then look for a developing path curling left and up to the summit of this sharp knoll. It's short and very steep, so take time for a breather or two.

The way off the summit is west towards Chrome Hill. Look for the thin path immediately left of the ridge of Parkhouse Hill and carefully negotiate a way down this. It soon crosses to the right of the falling ridge-line, dropping steeply – this will be slippery in wet weather. Just above the final limestone pillar, turn back-right on a dirt path, then hard-left to reach the minor road which curls around the foot of the peaks up a shallow valley that breaches the hill-line here.

4. Turn right to approach a gate and cattle grid. Immediately before this, take the waymarked stile on the left, a concessionary path for Chrome Hill and High Edge. This instantly leads onto a steadily rising, grassy path up this wider southern nose of Chrome Hill. Persevere with the path, marked by white discs on posts. Once through a handgate near a sycamore tree the path steepens considerably before gaining the start of the summit ridge. This compact marvel is a series of stumpy pillars and knuckles of resistant limestone, reaching its highest prominence at this southernmost end of the rocky backbone. You've conquered the Dragon's Back!

Take a well-deserved rest here to digest the beautiful views at your feet, stretching way south down the Dove Valley, west across to the Staffordshire Moorlands and eastwards over further knolly terrain to a higher limestone edge that completely hides some of England's largest quarries just beyond.

Keep ahead from the top, favouring the left side for a short while before drifting right, steeply down to join the line of a wall on your right. Bend left with this to reach a walled corner and a handgate. Join the field path beyond, again marked by white discs, alongside the fence to another handgate. Turn uphill as indicated; at the top go left to a gate and follow the field-top path through two gates to reach a farm access road well above a stand of trees at a gateway and cattle grid.

5. Don't cross the grid; rather, bear half-left on a fingerposted field path for Booth Farm. Some very thin squeeze-stiles take the walk to and through old walled pasture to reach a field road at a set of gates. Advance on this track to reach a tarred lane. Turn left; then shortly bend right to pass Booth Farm's buildings. Keep left on the 'No Through Road'

just beyond the old water troughs and redundant cattle grid, walking the hard-surfaced track to reach a remote cottage at Leycote. Here, join the unexpectedly blue-signed old County Road, marked by a width-restriction sign. This walled way presently zigzags increasingly steeply as a marvellously preserved packhorse road, reaching a glorious little arched bridge over the Dove.

6. Immediately over the bridge, look left for a stile and path signed for Hollinsclough. Cross the nearby slab-bridge and turn left. A thin, damp, ledged path wends above the river through scrubby woodland to pass a secluded small barn. Here, rise up the hillside slightly to find a wider track joining obliquely down from the right. Walk ahead on this, along the break of slope. For 400m the way is indistinct; simply contour-walk, keeping a little above the line of tumbled wall on your left and don't drop downhill. Step over a brook in a strand of trees, beyond which the way gradually becomes clearer. Dropping slightly through thin woodland, a stile through a sloping wall beneath trees confirms you're on course. When a farm complex appears ahead, aim towards this to join the lane down to Hollinsclough.

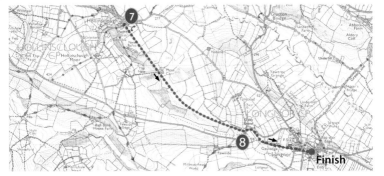

7. The view across the handkerchief-sized green here to the profile of Chrome Hill is exquisite. The building with the bell turret is the village school, built by the local landowner in 1840 as both schoolhouse and chapel of ease, essentially the village church. Go forward by the green on the lane past the telephone box and village noticeboard. It's now simply a matter of pounding this tranquil byroad between rough old walled pastures. Great views of the hills you conquered earlier offer a fine panorama as the lane undulates easily, gaining a little height before losing it again to reach, in 2km, a T-junction.

8. Turn left for Longnor; bend right and start uphill. In under 100m, opposite the village sign for Longnor, look for the possibly somewhat overgrown stile on the right – there's a fingerpost here too. Turn left along the top of the pasture; it's a distinct notched path across the slope. Ahead you'll soon see a large barn; before this is an offset wall corner and slim gap-stile (NB – this isn't the gap-stile through the long wall down to the right). Use this, and a handgate past the barn, then drift left to a handgate into the farm driveway. Turn right and walk into Longnor; keep ahead to return to the square.

The village found brief fame as the location for the television drama *Peak Practice* in the 1990s when it was rechristened as 'Cardale'. Somewhat earlier, it is believed that Jane Austen, residing for a time in Bakewell, used Longnor as the basis for the village of Lambton in her renowned novel *Pride and Prejudice*. In the churchyard at St Bartholomew's is a memorial stone to William Billinge, who died, aged 112, in 1791 after a memorable military career.

To old quarries, fabulous viewpoints and fascinating heritage on the western fringe of the Dark Peak.

The River Goyt and its tributaries cleave deep valleys into the bilberry-clad gritstone moors along the edge of which the Peak District's boundary meanders. This ramble makes the most of this terrain, offering a long series of magnificent views as it threads towards the bulky horizon of Kinder Scout's lofty plateau. The return is along country lanes and past a string of industrial centres now largely lost to history.

The walk commences from the wharves at Buxworth (or Bugsworth). This remarkable complex is the only surviving canal/tramway interchange in the country. Here, gritstone quarried locally and huge amounts of limestone from Dove Holes was transferred from the horse-drawn wagons of the Peak Forest Tramway to barges on the Peak Forest Canal. From here the boats headed for Manchester and the network of canals centred there. Information boards detail the area's fascinating heritage; don't miss the opportunity to visit The Navigation Inn, which has absorbing old photographs and plans of the site.

Paths and byways rise to a steep moorside lane, off which stony ways climb to mellowed old quarries at Cracken Edge and Chinley Churn. From this modest ridge are extensive views in all directions before a gentle descent to a gap in the ridge at Peep-o-Day. Near here, the Pennine Bridleway is joined for a while. This traces the route of one of the old packhorse trails across these fractured moorland expanses, picking a route below rounded tops. One of these is South Head, a distinct knoll in this secluded area of countryside where gritstone meets limestone; Dark Peak meets White Peak.

Leaving the Bridleway, a very rough lane drops past remote farms and through enclaves of tranquil haymeadows to reach Chapel Milton, an industrial hamlet on the fringe of Chapel-en-le-Frith. Sturdy viaducts stride across the Black Brook; this walk strikes down the valley, picking up waymarking for the Tramway Trail. This recalls the old iron plateway, which above Chapel Milton used one

of a series of inclines to link the upland quarries to Buxworth. The level line we'll soon follow was built as a tramway, but was originally planned as the upper end of the canal, scheduled to terminate at Chapel Milton.

Beyond Whitehough the old tramway puts on a show, with stone sleepers still much in evidence and sidings that once led to limekilns. The Black Brook is accompanied back to Buxworth.

THE BASICS

Distance: 8½ miles / 13.7km

Gradient: Undulating, steep in a few places

Severity: Challenging

Approx. time to walk: 4¾ hours

Stiles: Around 14 stiles and gates

Map: OS Explorer OL1 (The Peak District: Dark Peak Area)

Path description: Tarred lanes, field and farm tracks and paths

Start Point: The Navigation Inn, Buxworth (GR SK 023821)

Parking: Roadside near the Navigation Inn (SK23 7NE)

Dog friendly: Only suitable for agile and fit dogs. On leads near main roads.

Public toilets: None

Nearest refreshment: Pubs at start and en route

Start

The Route

1. Put the pub to your right and walk up Brookside, over the Black Brook bridge and up to the nearby road junction. Bear right, passing the infants' school and War Memorial Club before rising below the double railway bridge. Stay with the main road to pass Dolly Lane in 100m. In a further 50m, at the terrace-end, fork left up the grassy track in front of Splash Lane End cottage. In another 50m, beside the close of houses (left), fork half-right up the path through the rough pasture. Beyond a field gate, join the sunken, walled, tree-lined track (which may be boggy), presently bending right beside the wall to a higher gate-side stile. Advance across the greensward, soon continuing ahead along a tarred lane which passes a stone buttress and then the Tithe Barn complex (left).

2. At the junction on a bend in 550m, turn left up the steepening road, soon passing Dry Clough Farm. Some 250m after the farm look carefully for the footpath back-right (the fingerpost and stile are high-up on the bank), which starts a steady rise onto Cracken Edge. Excellent views already take the eye, a portent of things to come. A second stile leads into Access Land; the path continues its gradual ascent, revealing a fine panorama to the north, and presently passes a little above a rusting old winch set in a stone frame. This was the winding gear controlling an incline down which quarried stone – much used for roofing – was lowered on wagons; the route of the incline is seen dropping steeply into the valley of Otter Brook. The wagons initially continued to Chinley's busy station, but frequent derailments meant that horse-drawn working was more reliable!

Soon afterwards the path levels to strike through the abandoned quarries that gnawed away at Cracken Edge and Chinley Churn until they were closed in the 1930s. There's a combination of caverns and open workings here, so it's best to stick to the main path. As you approach the wooden stile at the northern end, fork left up the grassy path to find a stone-step stile 30m higher up the wall, formed around an old stone gatepost.

3. Once over this, walk ahead on the good path along the wide, reedy ridge-top, soon crossing through a tumbled wall-line. The reward for gaining these extra few feet is immense, with marvellous views opening out west across Cheshire and over Manchester city centre to the distant West Pennine Moors. To your right are sublime views across the distinct sharp hills of Mount Famine and South Head to the sculptured crags and edges of the Kinder massif.

Pass through a cross-wall at a waymarked gap (white arrow disc) and keep ahead, closing gradually to a wall off to your left. As you reach this at an offset left corner in 200m, cut ahead-right with the nearer wall-line, soon finding another white disc. Just past this look right for another disc by a cross-wall at a narrow handgate; use this and walk ahead to gain a wide, fenced path. Turn right and trace this bridleway down through the garden of the secluded house; continuing then to the main road at Peep-o-Day farm.

4. Turn left, cross carefully and go right up the rough track before the house. Beyond an old quarry this meets a wide cross-way; turn right up this, the route of the Pennine Bridleway for South Head. A long steady climb ensues; the National Trail is adequately waymarked, bending left before the first obvious gate and then passing through two offset bridlegates at a small corral before continuing as a braided way through another gate into the National Trust's High Peak Estate, advancing around the snout of South Head. -

To your left the deep little valley of Dimpus Clough slides below the slopes of Mount Famine, dropping into the Sett Valley's fringing meadows and the distant woods above Hayfield. The looming moors mark the edge of Kinder Scout, with crags like Swine's Back and Three Knolls as guard-towers for the distant, shadowy wall of Kinder Low and Crowden. A short, steep path leads to the top of South Head if you're so-inclined!

The main track tops out beyond the Edale path junction (ignore), then falls through a gate out of the High Peak Estate to reach a junction of moorland roads. Off to your left, the squat stone tower is a ventilation shaft for the Cowburn railway tunnel.

5. Turn right at this junction down the walled track, Beet Lane. It's rough underfoot until Beet Farm is passed, where it becomes tarred. Remain with it for nearly 1km, passing the large barn complex at Slack House on your right. In another 150m turn left on a crossing tarred lane, soon dipping over  a brook before bending right and rising to pass the entrance to Gorsty Low Farm. Trace the lane over the railway, bend right then turn sharp-left on the lower road. In 50m take the gap-stile on the right, walking the path in trees then across a paddock to a rough track. Turn right to the main road at Chapel Milton.

6. Turn downhill and cross carefully in 50m into the driveway for Riverside House. Bear right on the tarred path ('Tramway Trail') to pass under the remarkable converging viaducts which towered over a large cotton mill here, demolished in 1947. The nearer viaduct dates from 1890 on a link to the Manchester to Sheffield Hope Valley line; the second from 1867 on the Manchester Central to London St Pancras line. Use the ladder-stile into a long pasture. Head for the distant buildings at Bridgeholm Green, where a very narrow gap-stile leads into a small industrial estate; the stone building here was a paper and textile mill.

    At the road go left and cross the Black Brook. Just before the bypass bridge, turn right on the concreted lane; within 60m keep left on the rougher way. You'll notice you're walking on stone blocks; these are the sleepers of the former Peak Forest Tramway, which carried limestone from moorland quarries at Dove Holes to Buxworth canal interchange between 1796 and 1925; information boards outline its history. The holes are where the rails, or plates, were attached. The gauge was 4ft 2ins; standard railway gauge is 4ft 8½ins. Passing the vast site of Forge Mill – originally a paper mill, latterly a bleachworks that specialised in bed-linen cloth – which was demolished in 2010, the way reaches a road at Whitehough.

7. Two fine pubs are 150m up to the left; otherwise cross into the continuing track along the bed of the old tramroad. Cross straight over the next lane and ahead over old stone sleepers, passing the lodge (lake) of another old mill on your right – look for the black swans here. Beyond the industrial buildings it's an agreeable wooded stroll along the old trackbed back to The Navigation Inn.

FROM THE EDALE VALLEY TO SCULPTURED STONES ON KINDER'S FABULOUS FRINGE.

The huge plateau of Kinder Scout is one of the most recognisable locations in the Dark Peak. This immense area of peat bog and cotton grass ripples to the horizons at a height of just over 2,000 feet (610m) making it, technically at least, a mountain. It's also amongst the highest land in the Peak District, separating the Vale of Edale from the picturesque Woodlands Valley.

Across it threads England's premier long-distance footpath, the Pennine Way National Trail, which starts its winding course northwards to Kirk Yetholm, in the Scottish Borders, from the modest village of Edale. The place is clustered at the foot of Grindsbrook Clough, where the Old Nags Head Inn marks the start of this challenging recreational trail. It's also a highly popular focus for rambles up onto the much-visited western section of the plateau.

This walk also commences from the village, but heads instead for the relatively tranquil acres of the far-eastern end of Kinder. The rewards are equally attractive, but shared with far fewer fellow ramblers on a round of cloughs, moors and ragged edges. What's more, there's a handy railway station on the Sheffield to Manchester main line, offering easy access all year round to this glorious corner of the National Park.

The walk first heads along the break of slope across the northern side of the Vale of Edale, passing a series of steep-sided cloughs, each one plugged by a farmhouse or country house sheltered in trees against the fearsome winter weather that sweeps from the plateau. Many are named booths, which comes from the Viking word for 'place of shelter' where sheep and shepherds could shelter from weather – or wolves!

Beyond Jaggers Clough the way starts upwards, partly along the course of a Roman Road across the moors, before topping out at the plateau edge at Crookstone Out Moor. Peaty paths strike to the heart of the plateau and the exposure of rocks called Madwoman's Stones. From here the edge is regained, starting a memorable stroll between and past a string of cliffs, crags and weather-deformed stones to reach the head of Grindsbrook Clough. This scimitar-like gash in the fringe is a fittingly grand conclusion to an exploration of Kinder. The return to The Old Nags Head and a welcome pint is either down the precipitous clough beside the tumbling beck or via the shapely Grindslow Knoll and a few steps on the Pennine Way.

(NB: check Access Land closure information – see p.2)

THE BASICS

Distance: 10 miles / 16km

Gradient: Several steady climbs, one steep descent

Severity: Challenging

Approx. time to walk: 6 hours

Stiles: Three or four plus numerous gates

Map: OS Explorer OL1 (The Peak District: Dark Peak Area)

Path description: Tarred lanes, paths and tracks, some rough moorland paths, awkward in places

Start Point: Edale car park/railway station (GR SK 124854)

Parking: Edale National Park Car Park (pay and display) (S33 7ZP)

Dog friendly: Only suitable for agile and fit dogs

Public toilets: Edale

Nearest refreshment: Cafés, tearooms and pubs at Edale

Daily trains to Edale from Sheffield and Manchester (Traveline tel: 0871 200 2233)

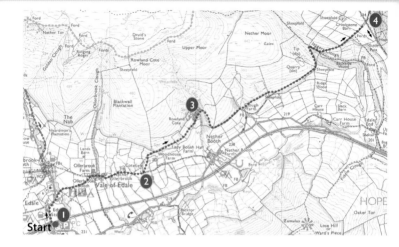

The Route

1. Walk up the lane from the railway station, heading north towards the great wall of moor that rises steeply behind Edale's houses. Pass the Moorland Visitor Centre and continue another 75m to the graveyard on your
right. Turn right along the waymarked, tarred path here, skirting the walled burial ground and, beyond trees, following a field-side path to the hamlet of Ollerbrook Booth. Enter the farmyard and ease right, joining a tarred lane. Beyond the cottages remain on the lane, with a fingerpost for 'Youth Hostel', until it curves left to Cotefield Farm. Branch off ahead here on the waymarked track below the buildings and follow this through three handgates.

2. Immediately past the third handgate, turn left (signed) up the pasture, heading for the top of the stand of woodland sheltering Woodhouse Farm. Skirt above this copse, entering Access Land and then along a pronounced path around the hill-slope to reach the complex of buildings at Rowland Cote. Nowadays a Youth Hostel, this was largely built as a grand Victorian villa on the site of a farm that was part of the Duke of Devonshire's estate.

3. Head for the far end of the main building. Just above and off the sharp driveway bend, drop right to cross the footbridge over Lady Booth Brook into the National Trust's Nether Moor estate. The path eases gently around the hill snout to run beside a stone wall to the stand of trees above Clough Farm. Step over the stream and stile and advance, initially steeply, again just above a wall. Presently, merge with a wide moorland track rising steadily along this northern flank of the Noe Valley to reach the thick woods smothering Jaggers Clough. Drop around the hairpin bend above

the woods, then continue through the gate and ford on the rising track. Use another gate and advance to reach a cross-track marked by countless directional posts.

4. Here the way is left. A short diversion to the right, however, finds the Hope Cross. Dated 1737, it may stand on the site of a medieval waymarker cross on the ancient track across the tops. Turn back to the crossways and keep uphill, signed for 'Glossop via Snake Pass'. In the trees to your left is Crookstone Barn, a secluded outdoor centre in a farm dating back to Georgian days.

This short section of route follows the probable course of the Roman Road built to link the forts at Navio (today's Brough, near Hope) and Melandra (near to Glossop), essentially today's tortuous Snake Pass road between Glossop and the Upper Derwent Valley. It's part of the Doctor's Gate route between Sheffield and Manchester, named after a Dr Talbot, who owned much land hereabouts and was responsible for the upkeep of the track in the years around AD 1500 to 1550.

Trace the old track to and through a gate in 300m. Here, turn left onto the thinner, grassy track to start a steady ascent up the flank of Crookstone Hill. Bear right at the carved waymarker stone near two stunted sycamores – look back for glimpses of Ladybower Reservoir deep in Woodlands Valley – then go through a gate in a cross-wall. Beyond this the land roughens and the path presently steepens to scurry up a crag; keep ahead beyond this on the virtually level path near the edge. In 200m you'll reach a distinctive flat-topped and layered rock, effectively high above the top of Jaggers Clough and 50m before you'd reach a broken wall.

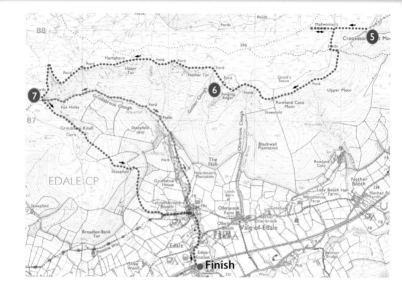

5. Here, fork ahead-right on the narrower path away from the edge. In 400m this reaches a huge rock split into a four-leaf-clover shape. Keep directly ahead, heading across the boggy moor to the distinctive rocks of the Madwoman's Stones 400m away. The origin of the name remains a mystery; they are simply one of many weirdly shaped or eroded formations scattered across the Kinder Plateau. Views are tremendous, particularly north to Bleaklow and east across to Derwent Edge.

    The plateau, crags and cloughs are a National Nature Reserve, designated in 2009 for its fragile ecosystem and the presence of rare and threatened species. Birds such as golden plover, twite, merlin, short-eared owl and ring ouzel are specialists of such upland areas. If you're here in spring, then keep half an eye out for mountain hares, which retain their white coats for a time after the snows have melted and thus show up very well.

    You may also see groups working to revitalise and replant huge areas of the upland heather moors that have become degraded over the past 150 years due to pollution. Re-seeding with heather and planting cotton grass plugs is planned to reverse the damage done and make the moors fit for the future as a resource for carbon capture and to protect the water-supply capabilities of these uplands.

    Return to the clover-leaf stone and turn right, joining a firm path south. This presently dips through a gully; in a further 400m it merges with the main path a little way away from the plateau edge. You'll reach the rocky buttress of Ringing Roger; the main path skirts away from the edge, passing through a line of cairns and well right of a lone little pine tree. At any splits, essentially remain on the level; at one point you'll pass close to the corner of a fenced area.

6. This immense buttress is the first of a series which the path, paved in sections, now skirts over the next 2km. Nether Tor, Upper Tor and Hartshorn just three of the named crags which lunge out over the deep gash of Grindsbrook Clough, the dramatic gulch down to your left. Soon after a handgate, the path curls right to use a hairpin above a sharp, slabby cleft, doubling back to reach the head of the Clough at a large area of bare bedrock and an enormous cairn.

7. It looks very daunting at first glance, but the precipitous path left, down into Grindsbrook Clough, soon becomes a rough-underfoot trail beside the beck. The well-worn route was the original course of the Pennine Way; it's still popular and reaches Edale just a short distance above the Old Nags Head.

A less severe return can be made via Grindslow Knoll. Instead of plunging down into the Clough, follow the higher path off to the left (with the Clough down to your left), passing behind a mushroom-shaped rock and heading to the crown of the Knoll and another large cairn 500m away. Walk ahead from the cairn 20 paces and look half-left for the handgate through a fence at the break of slope below; it's a steep descent to it. From this, a rough, wide path threads across the ghostly remnants of old pastures. Bending right above a wood, it becomes a grassy path beyond a gate and drops gently to join the current Pennine Way near a fingerpost and handgate. Bear left to emerge opposite the Old Nags Head Inn.

Turn down the lane to return to the car park and railway station 600m away.

Explore the now-extinct millstone quarrying industry amidst Hathersage Moor and Padley Gorge, with millennia of heritage along the way.

The eastern moors and edges of the Dark Peak are superb walking territory at any time of year. This energetic ramble starts high on the moors to the west of Sheffield and skirts along the crags and rocks at Burbage Moor. It's a magnificent amble high above the clough of Burbage Brook before entering the huge estate owned by the National Trust, which ripples across the moors and glens of this fractured, woodland-rich countryside.

The Longshaw Estate was the hunting preserve of the Dukes of Rutland until the late 1920s. It was purchased from the family by public subscription, largely thanks to the people of Sheffield who supported an appeal to raise funds to guarantee access to the city's nearby countryside. The whole estate and grand shooting lodge passed into the care of the National Trust in 1931. The route accompanies Burbage Brook into the deep cleft of Padley Gorge. This long gash into the thick deposits of millstone grit rock is soon clothed in marvellous old birch and oak woodland. This is a precious survival of such upland woods that once covered much of the Dark Peak and is renowned for its birdlife, fungi and a good number of butterflies.

Reaching Upper Padley, there's chance for a cuppa at a renowned ramblers' café at Grindleford Station before the route loops back past medieval Padley Chapel, where Catholic sympathisers worshipped during the persecutions of Elizabethan England and priests came to an untimely end.

The nearby quarries at Bolehill employed well over 400 people who quarried and worked more than 1.3 million tons of stone between 1901 and 1914. The millstone grit (so called because of its use as millstones) was particularly suitable for building the dams in the Derwent Valley above Bamford, as it hardened considerably after quarrying, making it good for dam construction.

Millstones were quarried around here from at least the 1440s; along the way are many that didn't make it beyond the quarries where they were first dug. The walk breaks free of these fascinating reminders at Millstone Edge, coursing then across gritstone tors and craggy exposures to reach the atmospheric site of Carl Wark Fort. This puzzling, enigmatic enclosure remains an unsolved mystery of archaeology; an archaic location with some magnificent views deep into the National Park. Nearby Higger Tor's bold horseshoe of crags is a final flourish en route to the finish line.

(NB: check Access Land closure information – see p.2)

THE BASICS

Distance: 7 miles / 11.3km

Gradient: Undulating, with several steady climbs and some short, steep sections

Severity: Challenging

Approx. time to walk: 4 hours

Stiles: Around 10 stiles and handgates

Map: OS Explorer OL1 (The Peak District: Dark Peak Area) and OL24 (The Peak District: White Peak Area)

Path description: Moorland and woodland paths and tracks, very rough underfoot in places

Start Point: Upper Burbage Bridge, Ringinglow Road (GR SK 260830)

Parking: Free car park at Burbage Bridge (nearest postcode S32 1BR)

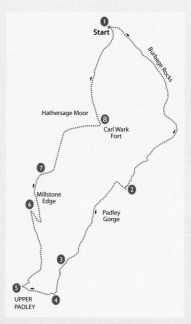

Dog friendly: Only suitable for agile and fit dogs. On leads near busy roads.

Public toilets: None

Nearest refreshment: Grindleford Station Café

The Route

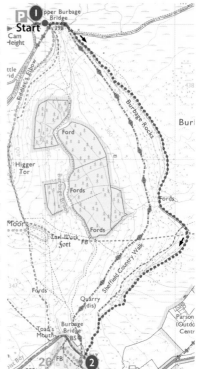

1. From the car park turn right, cross the bridge and walk round to the higher, roadside parking area. Find the furthest path on the right (not the metal kissing gate) and pick this up via a small handgate. The braided path strings along the crest of Burbage Rocks, passing above a small wood before dropping gradually to step across a stream. In a further 200m, beyond a deeply cut cross-path, bend easily right, continuing above the boulders and crags of Burbage South Edge to reach the main road at a small parking area.

2. Cross into the NT Longshaw Estate and turn immediately right on the grassy path parallel to the road. Once through a kissing gate, drop ahead onto a cobbled path that leads to a footbridge. Cross this; the path now slides downstream alongside Burbage Brook. Ignore the next footbridge; instead keep ahead to use a handgate into the woodlands of Padley Gorge. The path tumbles ahead across countless roots, whilst the brook cuts deeply down this steep, mossy, fern-fringed glen. Countless small falls and shoots bubble amidst the boulders far below, where dippers and wagtails bob in pursuit of food. Redstarts and pied flycatchers, treecreepers and nuthatches flit amidst the twisted boughs of the superb old sessile oak trees of Yarncliff Wood.

3. You'll reach a well-signed path (right) for Surprise View and Bolehill Quarry. Ignore this and continue on the current path another 250m. Look carefully then for the low waymark arrow (marked Longshaw longer route) pointing the way back-left. Take this; in 40m turn sharp right past a stone bench to find and cross a footbridge. Turn right up a few steps, then stick with the path as it soon again forks right to approach Burbage Brook. You'll soon pass above a gloomy, railed culvert where the brook is swallowed into a mill-race. Shortly afterwards is a gate into the lane at Padley Mill.

4. To reach the widely renowned station café bear left to cross the bridge. On your left is the western portal of the Totley railway tunnel on the Sheffield to

Manchester line; its 3½-mile (5.7km) bore was completed in 1893. Only the Channel Tunnel and the Severn Tunnel beneath the estuary between England and Wales are longer. Return over the bridge from the café and bend left with the roughening road, passing the former watermill that harnessed the power of Burbage Brook. Carry on past the houses, presently arriving at the mellow ruins of Padley Chapel.

The chapel is part of the ancient Padley Hall, built by the de Bernac family, who arrived in England with William the Conqueror. There was possibly a Saxon hall here for several centuries before. The chapel is renowned as the place where the Padley Martyrs Nicholas Garlick and Robert Ludlam were arrested in 1588; they were later executed at Derby. There's an annual pilgrimage to the chapel to celebrate their martyrdom, held each July on the Sunday nearest 12th July.

5. Continue on the track past the chapel and the few houses here to reach a cattle
    grid and a National Trust sign. Immediately over the grid, turn right through a
    handgate (not the grassy path) onto a wall-side path up into the woods. As the
    wall turns away right in 100m, turn left on a crossing path and walk this for 50m
    to find the line of a former industrial railway. This is slightly indistinct; look right for
    the steep grassy slope. The incline linked the quarries on Bole Hill with the main
    line at Grindleford sidings. The stone was quarried to be used in the construction
    of the huge Howden and Derwent Dams in the years immediately before the Great
    War.

    Walk up the incline, passing a large stone block. You'll soon reach the site of
    the winding drum which controlled the wagons on which the stone was lowered.
    Pass right of the stone structure; then in 25 paces turn left up the continuing
    path, initially steep and rough. Stay with this as it strikes across two level grassy
    plateaux within the vast site of Bole Hill workings. Pass through a handgate and
    advance 50m to a fork. Here, turn left up the wider track and pursue this gentle,
    grassy course through superb birch woods to reach the higher parts of Bolehill
    Quarry.

    This is liberally scattered with millstones in various states of preparation. Some
    were destined for flourmills throughout the country, but never made it from the
    production line. These millstone grit stones tended to produce a greyish colour to
    the flour. A superior source of non-discolouring stones was developed in France
    and severely damaged the industry here which had been producing stones for

600 years. Another market was the famous cutlery industry in Sheffield, where stones were used until synthetic replacements appeared in the 1930s. Continue on the track all the way to the main road.

6.   Turn right and walk up the pavement to and around the sharp bend. On your right here is a fingerposted path. Pass this by and immediately look left for a field gate and fence line heading up to the heathery moors. Very carefully (it's a busy road) cross to this and keep the fence to your right for 100m. Use a handgate and put the continuing fence on your left. A rutted path now charts a course above the cliffs and crags of Millstone Edge, a renowned training area for climbers. Off to your right is the isolated stack of rock, the Mother Cap. Remain with the fence-side path for about 750m to a simple, low step-stile on your left.

7.   Ignore this; instead turn right by the slabby rocks and keep ahead up to the tumbled crags and boulders of Over Owler Tor. Turn left (as you approached) on the well-worn, wide path that heads north across Hathersage Moor, presently dropping straight across the shallow pass of Winyard's Nick. When you reach, on your right, a large walled enclosure, turn towards this, passing to the right beside its short nearer edge. From the corner look ahead-right to sight a rocky outcrop 400m ahead and walk to this. In parts the way may be very soggy (particularly in wetter weeks), so take time to find the best route, always heading for the distinct blocky wall on the crag.

8.   The rocky outcrop is the mysterious Carl Wark hillfort, the history of which is still uncertain. It may have first been built in the Bronze Age, or was perhaps fortified in the Iron Age or created during the Roman period. Such intrigue simply adds to the attraction of the place. The way now is north on the good path to climb to the sharp crag of Higger Tor. Larger and higher than Carl Wark, it would have proved more difficult to fortify and defend. From the summit area look for the continuing path which branches slightly right and follow this, well above the valley of Burbage Brook to your right, back to the car park at Upper Burbage.

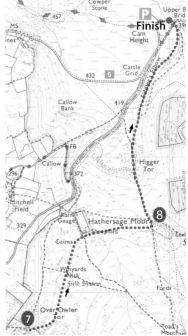

FOLLOW OLD PACKHORSE TRAILS AND SALTWAYS TO SHAPELY
SHUTLINGSLOE, COMMANDING REMOTE COUNTRYSIDE ABOVE
ANCIENT FOREST.

East of the Cheshire Plain, an intricate series of gritstone ridges, green vales and moorland domes form the western edge of the Peak District. Some of Cheshire's unsung rivers, such as the Dane, Dean and Bollin, spring to life in this challenging terrain, draining Cheshire's highest land down deep-cut cloughs that nibble vigorously into the looming mosses and steep scarps that characterise the area. This energetic walk sweeps through this beautiful, often secluded terrain, along the way encountering long-gone industries, a brace of country pubs and one of the Peak District's shapeliest summits, towering above moor, forest and vale.

The route commences beside one of the reservoirs that store the high rainfall this hilly terrain receives; water destined for consumers in Macclesfield, a couple of miles away. Old tracks thread up beside a tributary of the Bollin, clinging to the foot of the abrupt ridge of Tegg's Nose. Woods and steep pastures partially soften the stone quarrying that chipped away at this immense snout of gritstone until the 1950s. Stone from here was shipped as far as the Isle of Man to be used in municipal parks and gardens in Douglas. The old packhorse trail climbs steadily to meet the infamous Cat and Fiddle Road before diverging away along Charity Lane, part of a complex system of pack-routes and saltways that criss-cross the Peaks.

The lane reaches the modern plantations of Macclesfield Forest. This was once prime Royal Forest hunting country; the woods and chases of the Angevin Kings now depleted to valley oak woods and remnant stands of broadleaf woodland, a mottled baize of green

clothing the steep slopes and sharp valleys at the source of the River Bollin. At Forest Chapel is a tiny church where the ancient practice of rushbearing still occurs each August. An undulating woodland and moorland route now heads for the distinctive summit of Shutlingsloe. This shapely peak is nicknamed the Cheshire Matterhorn, its angular head rising above moors and wildflower-rich pastures which enfold the hamlet of Wildboarclough.

The old mills here are long gone, closed in the 1860s. The village name may well refer to wild hogs hunted hereabouts by the Earls of Derby in medieval times. Such hunts are long in the past; today it's a tranquil, peaceful countryside which leads into hidden Oaken Clough, heralding a return to the reservoir-spattered heart of the forest.

THE BASICS

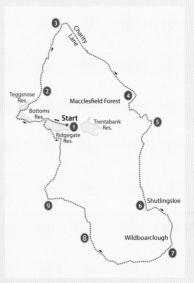

Distance: 11½ miles / 18.5km

Gradient: Plenty of climbing; one steep ascent and descent

Severity: Challenging

Approx. time to walk: 6½ to 7 hours

Stiles: At least 12 plus handgates

Map: OS Explorer OL24 (The Peak District: White Peak Area)

Path description: Tarred lanes, farm roads, field, woodland and moorland paths and tracks

Start Point: Ridgegate Reservoir, Langley (GR SJ 957715)

Parking: Waterside pull-in at Ridgegate, 500m east of Leather's Smithy pub (SK11 0NE)

Dog friendly: Only suitable for agile and fit dogs. On leads near busy roads.

Public toilets: None

Nearest refreshment: Pubs near start and on route (generally closed most weekday afternoons)

The Route

1. From the lane-side parking, head back to the Leather's Smithy pub and bear left, downhill, to reach Bottoms Reservoir. Opposite the terrace of cottages, slip right into the waterside track, then cross the dam. Beyond the footbridge at the far end, turn right along the track beside Teggsnose Reservoir, from which there are good views to the wooded acres of Macclesfield Forest.

2. Just before a field-edge gate closes this track in 800m, fork left and cross the stepping stones, climbing then on the rough track across the lower flank of Tegg's Nose hill. On reaching the tarred lane, at a sharp bend by the top of a rough farm drive, turn left and accompany this rarely trafficked way up to the main road at Walker Barn, a gentle 1.2km climb.

3. Turn right along this often busy road – there's a wider verge opposite. At the Peak District boundary marker (a millstone) in 100m, fork right up Charity Lane, continuing the gradual climb. Immediately after this bends sharply right, turn left on the rougher track rising easily outside the forest edge. Immense views are revealed north up the line of the South Pennines, and west both to the West Pennine Moors beyond the centre of Manchester, just 17 crow-miles (27km) away, and the Cheshire Plain, with the great disc of Jodrell Bank telescope perhaps glinting in the sun. Beyond the track's crest (at 477m the highest point of Macclesfield Forest), the imposing ridge of Cat and Fiddle Moor – England's second-highest pub is beside the distant hill-top transmitters – and Shining Tor, the highest point in Cheshire, create the horizon. The hollow way drops towards the deep green vale of Wildboarclough.

4. At the hamlet of Forest Chapel, where St Stephen's Church hosts a rushbearing ceremony each August, turn right on the tarred lane past Toot Hill House. At the Forest's edge in 400m, go left through the handgate at the fingerpost, dropping to a path junction at a fenced corner in

150m. Go left for 'Standing Stone', a winding woodland path with a long section of boardwalk over the headwaters of the River Bollin, climbing steeply to the forest car park at Standing Stone, reached by turning right once out of the woods. Turn right to the nearby road junction; from here choose the gated gravel track opposite.

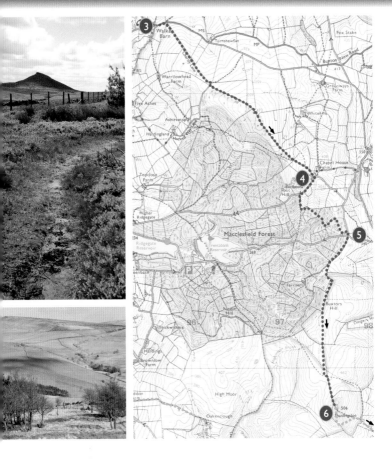

5.   Advance for 350m; then fork left beside a small pond onto a waymarked concessionary path. Keep the Access Land boundary fence to your left, rising with the braided path through an area of immature maples. The walked, waymarked route crosses through a tumbled wall several times before toying with a wall/fence-side path. The pyramidal peak of Shutlingsloe creates an eye-catching horizon; the path presently reaches a wide, low stile at a fenced corner. Climb this and keep ahead on the path beside the fallen wall, in time going through a handgate at the corner of Piggford Moor.

Stay true to the path directly towards Shutlingsloe, partly along a webbing reinforced route over boggy ground. You'll reach a slabbed path immediately before a kissing gate. Head now up Shutlingsloe, through the gate and then up the high stile/gate; then steeply up the paved, stepped path to the summit. Views can be immense, taking in the Clwydian and Berwyn Mountains to the west, The Wrekin, Long Mynd and Clee Hills to the south, and wide views across the Manchester Basin to the West Pennines to the north.

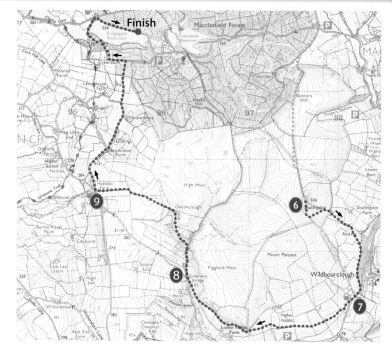

6. Walk past the triangulation pillar and along the short summit plateau. As it narrows and fails, turn left on the initially steep path down the flank of the hill, essentially heading to the right of the farm below. The way passes through a couple of gates/ stiles to gain a driveway. Turn right  along this, above bluebell-spattered woods to reach the lane in the valley of Clough Brook; here keep right to the nearby Crag Inn at tiny Wildboarclough. This once served workers at carpet and calico printing mills that thrived until the 1860s just upstream in this unlikely rural spot.

7. Look for the small handgate beside a field gate at the bottom of the pub car park. Once in the sloping pasture bear left to skim through the top of the scrubby gorse to find a handgate maybe 50m right of the lower field gate. This is the first of five which take the field path very gradually uphill across a succession of pastures. The way passes 120m below the stone barn; then well below the farm at Higher Nabbs. Each gate is well marked by a very large red disc. Below the farm, cross the brook and walk ahead, gradually easing right over a stile above scrub before reaching a step-stile into the lane which curls across the hillside. Turn left on the lane and at the junction keep ahead to reach Greenway Bridge in another 220m.

8. Immediately before it, take the signed path right, through a kissing gate and along the slope above Highmoor Brook. Cross a footbridge beyond a handgate, then continue gradually left on the well-marked path up the shallowing valley to approach the grounds surrounding the Arts and Crafts style country house hidden away in Oaken Clough. The waymarked path skirts well to the left of it, past a pond to reach the driveway.

    Cross diagonally to join the wall-side path, a short and steep climb to reach a handgate. Once through this, leave the wall and walk ahead on a grassy trod which passes just right of reedy upland ponds before joining the line of a tumbled wall on your right. At corner stone gateposts, jink right; then use the nearby stile into the enclosed track left, dropping with this to a lane at The Hanging Gate pub. The benign pub sign disguises the name's origins – it was where poachers caught in Macclesfield Forest were hung at the gateway to this Royal domain!

9. Turn right on the lane and keep ahead at the facing junction; the lane is soon marked as a 'Quiet Lane'. With Tegg's Nose and Macclesfield Forest forming the horizon, simply remain on this for over 1km and past several cottages. Keep right at the junction beside the driveway to Thickwithens Farm, dropping to reach a sharp-right bend at a hill-foot.

    Take the forestry track to the left here, advancing through the woodland fringe for 200m before the well-surfaced wide path (shared with mountain bikers) drops through the woods to reach a wider path beside the reservoir. Turn left on this, which loops left past a valve-house enclosure before bending right as a way across the foot of the grassy dam at Ridgegate. Turn right at the Leather's Smithy pub and retrace the outward section back to the start.

WONDERFUL WILDFLOWERS, ANCIENT FIELDS, TRANQUIL VILLAGES AND SPECTACULAR GORGES AT THE HEART OF THE WHITE PEAK.

Just east of Buxton, the Derbyshire Wye has created a string of deep, twisting canyons through a memorable landscape of crags and woodlands. Above this mayhem, the tranquil village of Chelmorton slumbers amidst its fretwork of ancient haymeadows, secluded along country lanes in a rolling landscape of hamlets and farmsteads.

This walk commences beside the Wye and heads towards a massive quarry complex. Appearances deceive; just behind the industrial scars is the most delightful, secret dale hosting one of the very best wildflower displays anywhere in the National Park. The walk strides up this rift in the landscape to emerge onto the plateau near Chelmorton. Tracks meander through the quilt of thin pastures here, which mirror the former open field system of medieval times. It's an easy stroll to the heart of the village, with its cosy inn and sturdy church standing opposite each other as the village lane gives way to rough byways into the limestone uplands.

Old mining tracks are then pursued across the plateau, dropping to the hidden hamlet of Priestcliffe before heading via further old strip fields to descend steeply into the Wye Valley at Miller's Dale. The old station here is now one of the main access points to the Monsal Trail, a multi-user route along the trackbed of the old Midland Railway line between Manchester and London. We follow this for a short distance before deciding on the final section of the walk.

In lengthy wet weather the route back to the start is along the old line, through several tunnels and across towering viaducts giving some spectacular views of the Wye's twisting gorge, which is impassable after heavy rain. The dry-weather route drops from one of the viaducts down to the river, picking up a delectable waterside walk deep within the gorge. Several stretches of stepping stones explain why the route isn't usable at high water. It's an adventurous, challenging walk beside – and occasionally along – the fast-flowing river, with some exquisite views of towering crags of gleaming limestone before the way eases for a wooded return to the start.

THE BASICS

Distance: 9 miles / 14.5km

Gradient: Several steady climbs and descents

Severity: Challenging

Approx. time to walk: 5½ to 6 hours

Stiles: About 10 plus 10 handgates

Map: OS Explorer OL24 (The Peak District: White Peak Area)

Path description: Field paths and tracks, tarred lanes, riverside paths; very uneven, muddy in places, many steep steps

Start Point: Topley Pike (GR SK 104725)

Parking: Peak National Park car park (pay and display) at Wyedale, off A6 (SK17 9TE)

Dog friendly: Only suitable for agile and fit dogs. On leads near busy roads.

Public toilets: Miller's Dale old station

This is the most difficult-underfoot walk in this book and is for confident walkers only. Expect very rough, uneven paths, steep and awkward natural limestone steps which can be slippery, lots of roots and heavy summer undergrowth. The rewards will repay the effort.

Nearest refreshment: Church Inn, Chelmorton; Waterloo Hotel at Priestcliffe turn (both close 3pm on weekday afternoons); snack bar at Blackwell Mill cycle hire (not winter)

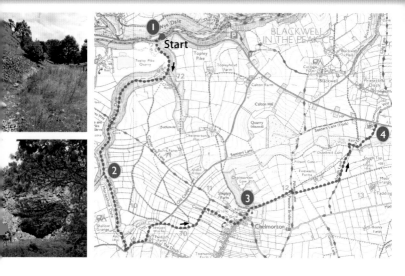

The Walk

1. From the Wyedale car park at Topley Pike, carefully cross the A6 to join the access road to the quarry; within 30 paces slip into the parallel fenced path on the left. Follow this (the roadway soon turns away) to a path junction in about 500m – there's a green cast-iron footpath sign in trees on your right. Turn right, through a handgate (signed Deepdale), and walk to the nearby information board. Climb the lengthy flight of steps here, then bend right on a stony path which drops easily past a grassy old slurry lagoon.

   This is soon left behind; beyond it Deepdale beckons. The path is generally very uneven underfoot, so take your time. For much of the year it's a dry valley, with any water flowing deep below ground in fissures and passages; in wetter years and winter months there's commonly a surface stream for at least the first half of the walk up the dale.

   During spring and summer, the dale becomes a kaleidoscope of shades and patterns as different flowers come to prominence. Cranesbill and rock rose, harebells and cowslips, bellflowers, mountain pansy and a variety of orchids are just a few to spot. In summer you'll be walking through head-high drifts of meadowsweet and great willowherb. The area is designated as a nature reserve.

   Natural screes plummet down the sheer sides, here and there added to by waste from small lead mines which have been worked periodically over the centuries. The wall on your right along the valley floor beside the streambed marks the boundary between two mining 'liberties', the archaic way by which Peak District lead mining was controlled, managed and licensed.

About halfway up the dale you'll see a large cave mouth up to your left, Thirst House Cave. Victorian excavators discovered the bones of bears here, while fragments of Romano-British pottery suggest that it was used as shelter 2,000 years ago. A lead vein was worked in the back of the cavern and given the name Spice Pudding Mine. Local lore makes it home to a hobgoblin with powers over the nearby spring. If you drink the waters on a Good Friday then all your ailments will disappear! Persevere along the dale-bottom path, presently climbing a stile out of the nature reserve.

2. The much-improved path reaches a dale split; bear left up Horseshoe Dale. You're walking the Priest's Path, named in favour of the curates of King Sterndale, a tiny village to the north, who used to 'commute' between the chapel here and the church in Chelmorton. In another 1km the path slips through gates by barns to reach the main road.

    Turn left and ignore the nearby Chelmorton turn. Just after the waterworks on your left in another 400m, take the fingerposted, walled track off the pull-in on your right. From its very far end, where it opens into pasture beside an enclosed clump of trees, head half-left to a gate-side step-stile and bear right onto the track. This passes through a landscape of small walled haymeadows which mirror the medieval earth-bank boundaries of the strip fields that once surrounded the village. In a few places like Chelmorton the old pattern is replicated by tightly packed walls, created here by an Enclosure Act of 1805. When the track reaches the tarred Common Lane, go right to Chelmorton's single street; here turn left to the pub and church at the top. The church, founded in AD 1111 and built on several levels, is the highest village church in Derbyshire and has an unusual locust-shaped weather vane.

3. Fork right above the pub along the stony bridleway. It's a steep haul past woods before the way levels out along a rake (line) of old lead workings. At the tarred Pillwell Lane turn right a few paces to find the waymarked path left over a stone stile (not the farm road). Head for the middle of the opposite wall and then pursue the path along three field edges to reach a walled track. Turn left on this and walk it for 1km, through several gates down to reach the main road beside The Waterloo inn.

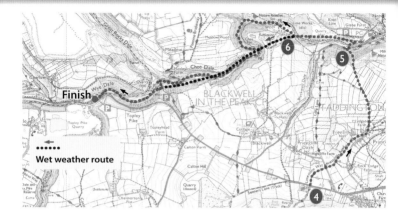

Wet weather route

4. Take the lane opposite through to the crossroads. Go straight over to reach the hamlet of Priestcliffe, where the tarred lane ends at a small green beside renovated barns at Lydgate Farm. The track you now need is left, signed for Millers Dale. In 500m it bends sharp left; here take the signed handgate on the right. Aim ahead to cross three meadows to find a corner handgate into a woodland nature reserve. The path drops down flights of occasionally very steep, narrow steps; at the bottom go left 50m to the main road at Miller's Dale.

5. Turn right; cross the nearby river bridge and take note of the state of the water. If it's flowing low and clear then the final section of the walk can be waterside. If it's high and muddy, then the last section is an elevated route. Once over the bridge turn immediately left to the nearby bend and take the stepped path up to the Monsal Trail (toilets and refreshment van are 150m right here at the old station). The way is left for Wyedale along the old railway to reach a viaduct just past the huge, concrete old East Buxton lime kilns.

6. At the far end of the viaduct is the parting of ways. *The wet weather option* means staying on the Monsal Trail through Chee Tor Tunnel, the first of several on this elevated passage up Wyedale offering an eagle's eye view of the deep wooded gorge. You'll eventually (1.75km) reach an 'End of Trail' sign at a gate; drop left here down to the lane above Blackwell Mill that heads upstream beside the river to return to the start.

The fine weather option means, once across the viaduct, you take the gated path to the right, signed for Blackwell and Chee Dale. This drops to a footbridge over the river; cross and turn upstream. *If the stones of the weir 40m upstream are completely underwater, then turn back and use the railway route to Blackwell*. This is the start of an enchanting, challenging ramble up the sublime limestone gorge. In summer the butterbur plants can be eye-level. Highlights include the voluminous Wormhill Springs which are soon reached. The way stays close to the river except for a dog-leg to bypass these springs. Don't be tempted up to the right 200m after – use the thinner, awkward and steeper path back down to the river!

Some sections drop down natural limestone steps and can be slippery. Two memorable stretches use stepping stones in the river beneath overhangs and along the base of buttresses popular with rock-climbers. Between these stretches the path crosses two footbridges – the river is always on your left except for the

short stretch between these Passing beneath several viaducts (ignore a third footbridge, left, beneath one), we'll presently reach the terrace of cottages at Blackwell Mill. Cross the footbridge and turn right up the level lane past the cycle-hire centre back to the start.

ABOUT THE AUTHOR

It was in the mid 1970s that Neil Coates first explored in detail parts of the Peak District. As a student of geography at the University of Keele, visits to some of the many and varied landscapes of the handy National Park became second nature – often accompanied by visits to some of the fine village and rural public houses which offered succour and shelter when need arose! Many of these happily survive well into the new century and offer pleasing and pleasant diversions to accompany his continued education in the area's nooks and crannies.

Since those far-off days he's lived and worked in various locations in and around the Peak District, getting to know more of the areas which generally eluded him in the 1970s. With a comprehensive background in the promotion of public transport, tourism marketing and magazine journalism featuring the area, his explorations continue apace, with new discoveries around almost every corner to add to a wealth of experience of the area's heritage and landscapes.

The selection of walks included in this book include elements of all these facets which make exploring the uplands and vales of Cheshire, Staffordshire, Derbyshire and the fringing Yorkshire Ridings such an absorbing pastime. A range of both well-known and little-visited locations take in most aspects of the natural and built environments that together make the Peak District a remarkable area to visit, enjoy and explore, fully justifying its designation as a National Park.

Neil lives on the Lancashire side of the Mersey Valley, just a stone's throw from some of the most challenging countryside the Peak District has to offer. His previous books for Bradwell include the Greater Manchester volume in the 'Walks for all Ages' series.